a flower bent
40 days of reflection

claudia

WESTBOW
PRESS®
A DIVISION OF THOMAS NELSON
& ZONDERVAN

WestBow Press books may be ordered through booksellers or by contacting:

WestBow Press
A Division of Thomas Nelson & Zondervan
1663 Liberty Drive
Bloomington, IN 47403
www.westbowpress.com
1 (866) 928-1240

Scripture quotations taken from THE HOLY BIBLE, NEW INTERNATIONAL VERSION®, NIV® Copyright © 1973, 1978, 1984, 2011 by Biblica, Inc.® Used by permission. All rights reserved worldwide.

ISBN: 978-1-9736-3623-6 (sc)
ISBN: 978-1-9736-3624-3 (e)

Library of Congress Control Number: 2018909327

Print information available on the last page.

WestBow Press rev. date: 9/4/2018

dedication

To Jumaani, Skaai and Canaan.

preface

Most of my songs are inspired by Bible verses, Bible stories or the wonderfully extravagant words of Jesus. Like the iconic butlers of film, I offer each song on a neatly-arranged tray. ("Your breakfast, sir").

In this compilation, each song is presented as a devotional thought for reflection and further study. My hope is that you will increase your understanding of God, His love and His plan for the world.

With some exceptions, these songs are recorded on four CD collections: "darkness into light" (2011), "barely audible" (2013), "a thousand singing birds" (2017) and "comfort" (2019). Ideally, while you read, you can listen to the songs for inspiration and insight.

God is real!
Thanks for listening and thanks for reading!

contents

introduction

Then he returned to his disciples and found them sleeping.

~ Matthew 26:40

They were to pray that they would not fall into temptation. Jesus prayed and persevered. The disciples did not, and they failed.

~ Bob Deffinbaugh

There is never a shortage of great ideas. Great ideas abound patiently in piles with other great ideas. Like a great pile of shoes in that game we used to play as kids, or the pile that forms in a recycle bin, or on middle school locker-clean-out days, or the can collection in a sophomore's dormitory window.

Over the years, I have accumulated plenty of piles. Like sorting laundry, each item gets tossed onto its likeness. Songs, stories, poems, expositions. No reason to stop there. I have a pile of friends I don't call, a pile of minutes I've wasted, a pile of words I regret and a pile of memories I've forgotten.

In the children's game, those worn and tattered shoes eventually rescued by their owners are precious treasure easily overlooked. Similarly, it's easy to overlook the treasure in our worn and tattered lives.

A disciple is one who commits to the discipline of learning; a student; one who wants to follow the discoveries this planet affords. Often, the word disciple is associated with the twelve disciples of Jesus. That's a good example and it suits the purposes of this book.

I believe that God speaks and speaks and speaks. He continues to reveal Himself; to send us hints and clues and illustrations. Some people may be more in tune to those frequencies than others yet, eventually, each person intersects with some aspect of God. Maybe it's through a song or a friend's kindness or a tragedy or by facing the monsters of disease and fear. Those moments may occur more often with some than others. If you are metaphorically sleeping, a lot happens without your awareness.

The term "sleeping disciples" alludes to the scene at the Garden of Gethsemane (Matthew 26:40) where Jesus faced his most crucial moment. His disciples were there. It was a significant event for them, too. But, where do we find them? Sleeping: like we who are overwhelmed with responsibilities, burdened by worries, worn down and tattered. They were sleeping when they should have been awake.

I was taught that God speaks through the Bible, in the "still small voice" when I kneel in prayer. The reality is that often there is not enough time to stop and have devotions. Prayers are hurled over speeding traffic; prayers ride falling tears that can be restrained no longer. Even when there is no time for devotions, formal Bible study or quiet time on your knees, God doesn't stop caring for you or sending you messages. He will always keep His promises (Isaiah 46:4). He cares even when we are unaware.

Consider the mushroom. Even if you don't like mushrooms, don't ever eat them, or can't stomach their smell, you must admit that mushrooms are readily available. There is never a shortage of mushrooms. When they are needed, they can be found. A lack of enthusiasm for mushrooms has absolutely no bearing on either their existence or their availability .

God is like mushrooms.

God's messages are like mushrooms. Your lack of interest, lack of enthusiasm or lack of time has no bearing whatsoever on the existence of God's messages or their availability. God still speaks to us. He always speaks to us. And not just to believers. He constantly sends messages reassuring the people on this planet that He exists, He cares and He is present among us in many ways.

Those who read the Bible are bombarded by those particular messages. So, if you don't like reading the Bible or don't have time to read the Bible, you are missing out on the constant barrage of messages that God has sent our way through sedulous preservation of Scripture. They tightly interweave to produce even more messages "between the lines" and literally between the letters. For example, the television station in our area sends out transmissions all day long but I have no clue what they are until I tune in. Wouldn't I be a fool to deny that those messages exist?

The Psalmist wrote, "The heavens declare the glory of God" (Psalm 19:1). Nature quietly and consistently carries messages from God and holds them for us like email or voicemail messages until you are ready to pick them up. Jesus quoted scripture in Luke 19:40 when he said, "If they keep quiet, the stones will cry out" (Isaiah 55:12 and Psalm 96:11). We, too, cannot be silent when we see glimpses of God. But even if we can, creation itself will find ways convey the message.

So, look around. Let the ideas in this book be the quiet tap on the shoulder that softly nudges you from your slumber, sleeping disciple. Or let it be the trumpet blast that wakes you from your blinding, numbing routine. Why even bother waking up? Why not remain sleeping? Because something great is going on around you. God cares about you and He is trying to reach you. Wake up sleeping disciple! Open your eyes. Look around. He wants to turn your blindness into sight and your darkness into light.

1

accendat in nobis sui amoris

There is nothing more truly artistic than to love people.

~ Vincent Van Gogh

To love another person is to see the face of God.

~ Victor Hugo

Accendat in nobis, Dominus
Ignem sui amoris
Et flammem aeternae caritatis
She sits alone in the dark
Hearing the echoes of a crowded room
When everyone has gone away
Tracing the circles on a faded chair
There's no one there
He walks alone through the park
Hearing the laughter of a child at play.
He wishes the sun would warm the gloom
Tries to remember why he's there
Does no one care?
They watch in wonder all day long
Hoping the next one will be theirs for sure
But there is silence in the night
They remember that it isn't fair
It's hard to bear
We sing and dance all night long
Believing another round will erase the pain
But how many times can we drown
Before we, ourselves, begin to fade?

It's too much to bear
Then an angel comes along
Beaming in radiant, sacred light
His arm is strong, his love is pure
Breaks the chains, throws away the fear
By the love he shares

Chicago airport, March 17, 2018, Air Canada flight loading at gate three at 5:30pm local time. On our walk in the corridor, a sprightly two-year-old raced out of a store merging inline with us. She ran happily as if she had a destination. Or maybe she was running away from something. Several seconds passed; more seconds than I was comfortable seeing a toddler on her own. Before concern turned to alarm, a father's arms at my knee level, snatched the girl and brought her back to her family group.

Having arrived at gate three, I stood watching the tide of passersby. Another young girl about five, skittered in front of me calling, "Mommy, mommy, mommy, mommy!" Again, a parentless child! But, not to worry. A woman in line about ten feet away called to the child, "I am here. Here I am." The girl flowed straight to her mother's leg and held on.

Minutes later, I heard crying and an insistent screaming. A tall, young father held his little girl in his large arms. She squirmed and wriggled and struggled to get from sitting in the bend of his arm to head down, diving towards the floor. As they passed me, I heard the father say, "Do you want to walk or do you want me to carry you?"

If Jesus had been standing with me, he would have told us a story (Luke 15).

Psalm 85:6-7

Will you not revive us again, that your people may rejoice in you?
Show us your unfailing love, Lord, and grant us your salvation.

Useless Resolutions

Are you in the habit of making resolutions? Especially New Year's resolutions? Some popular resolutions include losing weight, eating healthfully and joining a gym. Most resolutions have to do with eating better, looking better, feeling better, doing better. We are inundated with messages that appeal to our desire to improve ourselves and the quality of our lives.

Why do we use the term "resolution" anyway? We resolve to do better than we have been doing. Our resolution is in essence our determination to try again on the things that overwhelm us.

My resolution this year was the same as last year: to eat less chocolate. I say "less" because for years I've tried to eat no chocolate. - - Silence - - The fact that it is still my resolution indicates that I have not yet succeeded. Jesus said that without him we can do nothing (John 15:5). Not only that, what we do without him or outside of a faith relationship with him, is meaningless. No matter how determined I am, my power must come from Christ.

Jesus said he wants us to bear fruit (John 15:8). If we love him, we should keep his commandments. He goes on to tell us what the commandment is in a nutshell: Love each other. Care, courtesy, thoughtfulness, honesty, compassion, selflessness. Touch somebody, hold their hand, hold open a door, smile, speak kindly when you'd rather be as grumpy as you feel. Invite someone to participate in an activity with you. It's strange that Jesus doesn't ask us to accomplish great feats, leap tall buildings, join a health club and stop eating chocolate. He asks us to do all we can for the people we contact every day. Love each other (Matthew 26:37).

We are so determined at the beginning of a new year but all that determination ends in failure. Jesus has a different way. If we do what he commands, which is to love each other, then we will bear fruit. A tree doesn't resolve at the beginning of each new year to bear fruit and then spend the year striving to accomplish that goal. The fruit tree simply is a fruit tree and that's what fruit trees do. In saying, "I am the vine and you are the branches" (John 15:5), Jesus is saying: relax. Put away those accusatory resolutions. Just live in my power and you will bear fruit effortlessly. You can't do it on your own.

So, a new year's resolution? Forget it. Love each other. Everything else will come together; not by anything you do but by the power of Christ.

Prayer

Dear LORD, inasmuch as You have found me and love me, ignite in me Your love so that each day I will care for those whose paths intersect mine. May I be kind and gentle to those who are hurting. Let them find in me an expression of Your love. Let me be that angel who comes along and gives support and encouragement in times of loneliness and despair.

_____

_____

_____

_____

_____

2

a flower bent

> The violets in the mountains have
> broken the rocks.
>
> ~ Tennessee Williams

> The flower that follows the sun, does
> so even on cloudy days.
>
> ~ Robert Leighton

In the moment of my deepest, darkest night
When the stars refuse to shine
When the ground is parched and my strength is dry
And my thoughts are no longer mine
And there's no way through

Like a flower bent to the desert night
Holding on to moving sand
Desperately waiting for the sun
And there's no one to hold my hand
I turn to You

And I raise my head to the gentle rain and
I lift my eyes to see
The line of light to begin the day and
The rain falling down on me
I come to You

Learning quietly in my weakness I am strong
When I open my eyes to see

Waiting patiently now I found where I belong
Living water flowing out of me

And now I see
And now I am free
Alleluia

The way I see it, each of my songs is a window to a specific moment in my life. At the same time, a song is renewed each time I use my breath to give it life. Every time I sing this song, it reminds me that, in my weakness, I am strong not because of my ability but because of God's strength. "But he said to me, My grace is sufficient for you, for my power is made perfect in weakness. Therefore I will boast all the more gladly about my weaknesses, so that Christ's power may rest on me" (2 Corinthians 12: 9).

John 7: 37, 38

Let anyone who is thirsty come to me and drink. Whoever believes in me, as Scripture has said, rivers of living water will flow from within them.

Feast of Tabernacles

To really understand the above passage in John, we need to scratch a little deeper. By deeper, I mean the Feast of Tabernacles which in itself is layered with meaning. Every autumn, the Jewish Feast of Tabernacles, an eight-day festival, is celebrated around the world. It is also known as Sukkot or Feast of Booths. Moses instituted this festival over 3500 years ago to commemorate the years that the Israelites wandered in the desert after their Exodus from Egypt. Many Jews still celebrate it today by living outdoors in booths (or tents) through the festive period.

Jewish festivals are interesting on their own but their meanings are intriguing when viewed through the life and ministry of Jesus Christ. Jesus celebrated these feasts along with his people but, his life actually fulfills the feasts. For example, Jesus was crucified and died on Passover, one of the seven festivals. Passover is the very day that Moses instituted to remember that the lamb's blood saved the Israelites from death in Egypt. That is why we refer to Jesus as our passover lamb or the lamb of God who takes away the sins of the world (John 1:29).

The coming of the Holy Spirit and the birth of the Christian church occurred 50 days after Easter

Sunday, exactly on the same day of another festival given by God to Moses, the Festival of Weeks or Pentecost. All three Jewish spring festivals have an exact day-to-day match to later significant historical events that landed on festival days that were started over a thousand years before. This phenomenon is unique to Jewish history and is evidence of God's involvement in our history and in our world. In Isaiah (46:10), God declares that He is the only one who can tell us what will happen in the future. He has done that numerous times and in many ways, not only with verbal predictions but with the overlays of patterns that repeat in history with mathematical accuracy.

Those are the spring festivals. The fall festivals line up with eschatological events: days of warning and repentance, the day of judgement and the Feast of Tabernacles, a time of rejoicing when Jesus sets up his kingdom on earth. It was all foretold by words of the prophets and it is lived out by the festivals that Jews reenact every year.

Let's get back to Jesus at the Feast of Tabernacles. John records that Jesus participated in the Feast of Tabernacles but something strange happens. In John 7:37-39, on the last and greatest day of the festival, Jesus stood up and shouted that if anyone was thirsty, he should come to Jesus and drink and living water will flow out of him.

To appreciate these words, we need to keep in mind how the Jews celebrated on the last day of the festival and the significance of living water. Every day of the Feast of Tabernacles, priests and people descended the hill from the Temple to the spring of Shiloach, located down the hill from the Temple, and filled a golden flask with pure water. The entire crowd would ascend back to the Temple through the Water Gate singing Psalms 199-133 (which is why these psalms are called songs of Ascent). As the priests and people entered the gate with the flask of pure water, they would be met with the sound of the shofar or trumpets.

Once in the Temple, the priest carried the flask to the altar and poured it out. Isaiah 12:3, "With joy you shall draw water out of the wells of salvation," tells us that this ritual was carried out with joy and celebration. Sukkot, the Feast of Tabernacles as God tabernacles with men, is a time for great rejoicing because God dwells among us. We have the realization of the Divine Presence among us. Jesus used the context of the joyful gathering and pure water poured on the altar to identify himself as the one who gives living water to anyone who is thirsty. His hearers identified him immediately as Messiah. Why is that?

There are two key passages that help us make the connection. One in Jeremiah 2:13 "My people have committed two sins: They have forsaken me, the spring of living water, and have dug their own cisterns, broken cisterns that cannot hold water" and the other in Zechariah describing the Feast of Tabernacles and 'living water.'

In Jeremiah's words, we find the identity of God the Father. In Jesus' words, we hear that he identified himself as God. The Jews hearing Jesus speak would remember those words of Jeremiah. Jesus is making a direct statement about his divinity. Also, in Jeremiah 2:13, God referred to Himself as "the fountain of living waters." By calling himself the source of living waters, Jesus was indirectly asserting his divinity. As well, the Jews hearing Jesus speak these words would remember the following passage in Zechariah:

On that day his feet will stand on the Mount of Olives, east of Jerusalem, and the Mount of Olives will be split in two from east to west, forming a great valley, with half of the mountain moving north and half moving south...

On that day there will be neither sunlight nor cold, frosty darkness. It will be a unique day—a day known only to the Lord—with no distinction between day and night. When evening comes, there will be light. On that day *living water* will flow out from Jerusalem, half of it east to the Dead Sea and half of it west to the Mediterranean Sea, in summer and in winter. The Lord will be king over the whole earth. On that day there will be one Lord, and his name the only name. Then the survivors from all the nations that have attacked Jerusalem will go up year after year to worship the King, the Lord Almighty, and to celebrate the *Festival of Tabernacles*. If any of the peoples of the earth do not go up to Jerusalem to worship the King, the Lord Almighty, they will have no rain (Zechariah 14: 1 – 19).

Living water, Feast of Tabernacles, Messiah. Hearing Jesus talk about living water would have reminded the Jewish audience of this passage and they would have made the connection to Messiah.

The ancient 3500-year-old Feast of Tabernacles opens many layers of meaning, spanning history and theology, when considered through the person of Jesus Christ. Jews still celebrate the Feast of Tabernacles each year awaiting Messiah's glorious return.

Prayer

Father, there is nothing You do not know. In fact, You have ordained all things from the beginning, even arranging the times and the days. It is beyond our understanding. For that reason, I can trust You. I can trust that Your word is true. There is no need You cannot meet. There is no thirst You cannot quench. Please be to me that life-giving water as I lean heavily on You. There is no one else.

_____

_____

_____

_____

_____

3

all my longing

Prayer is not asking. It is a longing of the soul.

~ Mahatma Gandhi

In prayer, it is better to have a heart without words than words without a heart.

~ John Bunyan

Saviour, all my longing in Your loving bosom rings
My life, my desires, all my cares to You I bring
When all my strength fails and the light is extinguished from my eyes.
That's when Your salvation lifts me up with eagle wings.

Master, I will seek to live my life as You require
My days are but a vapour, like a memory they will expire
When again my foot slips and the pain is ever in my bones
Teach me Your deliverance give the strength that You inspire

All my longing is to rest within Your care
My assurance is to know that You are there
While I cling to You

Father, Your forgiveness more immense than I can understand
Lets You hear my prayer I respond when You lovingly command
You've become my tower Your peace is implanted in my heart
Thank You for your patience for securely holding my hand!

Between Abraham's story in Genesis 12 and the Israelites' exodus from Egypt are some intriguing alignments. In both stories, the males are in danger, there are plagues, Pharaoh sends them away, they leave with great wealth. In literature class, we would call Abraham's experience a foreshadowing of what would happen to Israel coming out of Egypt.

When Abraham lied to Pharaoh about Sarah, his wife, he showed his lack of trust in God. It is no wonder that after his Egyptian experience, Abraham is geographically between Beth-El and Hai (Genesis 13:3). There is a profound significance to his location evident by the Hebrew names that is not evident in English. That Abraham is between these two cities exposes his spiritual journey. Beth-El is the House of God and Hai is a heap of ruins. There he is, between one and the other, only a decision away from either destination. He could choose to continue in his own strength and experience the disaster that Egypt brought him or he could determine to stand on God's promise and take the path God ordained for him. Do we not find ourselves, with each problem that arises, one decision away from either destiny?

Psalm 38:9-22 (selected verses)

All my longings lie open before you, Lord;
my sighing is not hidden from you.
My heart pounds, my strength fails me;
even the light has gone from my eyes.
My friends and companions avoid me because of my wounds;
my neighbours stay far away.
Lord, I wait for you;
you will answer, Lord my God.
Lord, do not forsake me;
do not be far from me, my God.
Come quickly to help me,
my Lord and my Saviour.

Carbon Monoxide

Carbon monoxide is not poisonous. It is a killer because it usurps oxygen's rightful place. Hemoglobin, we know, is responsible for carrying oxygen in the blood. However, when carbon monoxide is present in the bloodstream, it binds itself to the hemoglobin in exactly the same location that the oxygen should be. Carbon monoxide wants the same spot in the blood that oxygen wants. If the carbon monoxide is present, the oxygen cannot occupy the same spot. What happens when you don't get oxygen? Exactly.

Carbon monoxide in the blood has a five times greater affinity to the hemoglobin than oxygen. That means it is pushier and bolder than the meek and mild oxygen. Hemoglobin is three times more likely to bind to carbon monoxide than to the oxygen. That means hemoglobin likes carbon monoxide just a bit more than it likes oxygen. We can better understand this by remembering that human nature prefers sweets over vegetables. Why are we tempted by milkshakes but not zucchini? Why are foods that may be detrimental more alluring than healthy choices?

In our family, we like to play a game called, "Would You Rather?" One presents two options and the other must make a choice. The following is a contrasting list to illustrate my point.

Would you rather . . . .
- eat broccoli or eat a brownie
- exercise or watch tv
- drink water or drink a carbonated beverage
- got to bed at 9:00pm or at midnight
- eat a salad or eat dessert
- save money or spend it
- buy an economy car or a sports car
- submit or fight

What we call human nature seemingly fights against itself. It is only by struggling against human nature that we live healthy lives. Perhaps we have either wrongly labelled those desires or we need a new nature (see Ezekiel 36:26). Our bodies willingly replace good, life-giving oxygen with the strangling contaminant carbon dioxide if it is present. There is no room for both. The best way to remain alive and healthy is to avoid exposure altogether.

The Western mind tends to dichotomize the idea of good and evil, holy and sinful, carnal and spiritual. These ideas hold that where there is good, evil cannot reside. Where there is holy, sin cannot abide. Perhaps this strict dichotomy and uncompromising duality comes from the concept of a holy, unchangeable God untainted by evil and untemptable by sin.

You cannot serve both God and money. You cannot be integral when courting both the desires that are opposed to God and the principals of love and compassion for others. You cannot have both. If you try, you will eventually flop to one side. As filling up the lungs with carbon monoxide depriving the body of oxygen will result in certain death, so will indulgence in evil and the abuse of self, others and the planet.

This is particularly poignant to a large portion of Christians, myself included, who believe that compromise is the way to navigate Christianity through a secular environment increasingly in opposition to our beliefs. You can make your own list of what concepts or pursuits take the place of God in the lives of Christians today. Which things lure you? Which things attract you? Which things usurp God's preeminence in your life? Furthermore, how do we address these issues personally and communally?

If we know that carbon monoxide attaches readily to hemoglobin depriving cells of much-needed oxygen when carbon monoxide is in the bloodstream, we should be vigilant to avoid situations where we breathe in carbon monoxide. Remember there is no battle between carbon monoxide and oxygen. It usurps oxygen's rightful place.

Prayer

My longings, my desires, they are all tied up in You Lord. Thank You for the opportunity to know You a little deeper in each stage of life.

_____

_____

_____

_____

_____

_____

4

a thousand singing birds

Prayer is not asking. Prayer is putting oneself in the hands of God, at
His disposition, and listening to His voice in the depth of our hearts.

~ Mother Teresa

If the only prayer you said was thank you, that would be enough.

~ Meister Eckhart

I don't know how to pray
I don't know what to say
I don't know what to do
I can't see my way through

I want to know how to pray
I want to know what to say
I want to know what to do
I want to see my way through to You

I can't explain
How I feel lost in the rain

A promise is a promise and Your promise is assured
You will wind around my heart where the hidden thoughts are heard
And like a thousand singing birds
A thousand singing birds
You will sing for me with sighs too deep for words

I've been a Christian a long time. I've prayed the pretty words of planned and scripted public prayers. And I've prayed in private through tears of confusion when words were ungraspable. God looks on the heart. Even better than that, since we have no idea what we are doing, God does it for us. Isn't that astounding? Another reason to rest in Him.

Romans 8:26, 27

In the same way, the Spirit helps us in our weakness. We do not know what we ought to pray for but the Spirit himself intercedes for us through wordless groans. And He who searches our hearts knows the mind of the Spirit, because the Spirit intercedes for God's people in accordance with the will of God. And we know that in all things God works for the good of those who love him, who have been called according to his purpose.

Fighting Our Battles

Neural pathways are carved into the brain by experience and repetition like wobbly cart wheels carve ruts into a muddy road. The longer you spend in an activity, the easier it is to slip back into those ruts. It is what it is. Life is difficult. But God made some promises and they are just as real. So, next time you get into a rut of your own making, claim one of His promises. He promised. He'll come through for you.

First of all, God knows we can't do this on our own. Secondly, He promised to do it for us. The Feasts in the Bible are "dress rehearsals" for real events to come and the stories in the Bible can also be layers of truth that apply to life in a broader sense. I'm going to tell you two stories in the Bible and then tell you what this can mean for you, too.

The first story is about King Jehoshaphat. He is the fourth King of Judah. He reigned from 872 - 878 BC. He reigned in Judah when King Ahab reigned in Israel. Jehoshaphat allied with Ahab who wanted him to go to war. Jehoshaphat wanted first to seek the counsel of the LORD before making a decision. Ahab assembled 400 prophets who counselled him to go to war. Jehoshaphat wasn't fooled. He asked if there were any prophets of Yahweh. Ahab's answer is comedic. He essentially said, "Yes, I have one but I hate him. He never says anything good about me," which tells you something about Ahab.

They went to war and Ahab died as Yahweh's prophet Micaiah had previously warned. Because Jehoshaphat was tangled in this mess, a large army was coming to Jerusalem for him. Alarmed, Jehoshaphat resolved to inquire of the LORD and he proclaimed a fast. He prayed something like this, "Yahweh, God of our ancestors, You rule. We are being attacked and we don't know what to do but, our eyes are on You!" That's a good prayer. Keep that in your pocket and use it often.

And this is what the the LORD, the Holy One of Israel replied, "Don't be afraid of them. The battle is not yours but YHVH's. Show up. Stand firm and see the deliverance YHVH will give you" (2 Chronicles 20:17). That's awesome.

The second story is about King Hezekiah. He was the thirteenth King of Judah and one of only three who did right in God's eyes. He reigned from 729-687 BC. Sennacherib the Assyrian, invaded Judah. Hezekiah's message to his people was: "Be strong and courageous, Don't be afraid or discouraged, There is a greater power with us than with him. YHVH our God is with us to fight our battles."

Sennacherib sent Hezekiah a letter ridiculing his faith in God and reminding him that other nations believed their gods would help them yet they, too, succumbed to the Assyrian power. Hezekiah took that letter, went to the Temple and spread it out before God. In essence, he was saying to God, "Look. Read this!" Of course, God answered Hezekiah and revealed His plans for Sennacherib. It all happened as God declared (2 Kings 18:1-19 and Isaiah 36).

I love those stories for two reasons. First, these men went straight to God. And second, God took over and fought their battles for them. I believe He will do the same for you if you ask Him.

Prayer

I'm so thankful that You fight our battles and that You will even pray on our behalf. What a wonderful Saviour.

_____

_____

_____

_____

_____

_____

5

a whispered rescue

> If you are renewed by grace, and were to meet your old self, I am sure you would be very anxious to get out of his company.
>
> ~ Charles Haddon Spurgeon

> Without renewal of mind, there is no transformation.
>
> ~ Lailah Gifty Akita

With eyes that see Your light
With ears that hear Your voice
With hands that hold each other's hands
And mind to make a choice

With hearts that feel Your pain
With lips that call Your name
With heads lifted to the dying rain
With heads bowed down in shame

We come before Your throne
To hear You call us Your own
Bleeding through time and all our tears
Renew our hearts again
Renew our hearts again

One cold winter day, there was a moment the sunlight shone through my living room window. That was beautiful especially since it had been so grey and dreary the previous few days. But, as I was enjoying the light, I realized that that beautiful light was accentuating all the dust that had accumulated on my shiny, black piano. Dust, that I did not notice in a darkened, shadowy room.

Minutes later, I got into my car. On a winter day, you might have to scrape the ice off a car's windshield. This morning, there were small crystals of ice across the windshield but I could see through them and I decided I didn't need to scrape the windshield. I pulled out of my shaded driveway into the sun. The light reflected off all those tiny ice crystals and I could not see through the windshield

In John 8, Jesus said, "I am the light of the world."

As I learned that winter day, light can do two contradictory things at the same time. In chapter eight of John's gospel, the light accentuated the sins of those who contrived to trap Jesus; those who needed to be exposed and corrected. Yet notice how Jesus protected (and forgave) the woman caught in the trap. He covered the sin of the woman. Jesus the light exposes sin in our heart that we should address and seek forgiveness for but, at the same time, Jesus the light asks us to be blind to the failings of others and forgive them as he forgives.

Amazing!

Psalm 51:10-12

Create in me a clean heart, O God, and renew a steadfast spirit within me. Do not cast me away from Your presence and do not take Your Holy Spirit from me. Restore me to the joy of Your salvation and sustain me with a willing spirit.

Entropy

Entropy is the gradual decline or deterioration into disorder. This is actually a complicated scientific equation but I don't need equations to convince me. Just live in my house for a week and you will see entropy in action!! Entropy is why we need these:

Toothbrush: A very handy and important tool to clean your teeth. If you eat a lot of sweets, you need it. If you eat only good food, organic vegetables and healthy options, you need it. Even if you eat nothing all day, by the end of the day, you need a toothbrush!

Soap: A great invention that cleans your body by breaking up oil and dirt into smaller bits that mix with water. Soap is made up of molecules with two different ends. One end attracts and sticks to water (hydrophilic) and the other end attracts and sticks to the dirt and oil (hydrophobic). Genius! If you roll around in the mud all day, you need it. If you spend a normal day, you need it. Even if you sat in a chair and didn't move all day, you would still need soap!

Shampoo: Cleans your hair. It works on the same principal as soap and it doesn't matter if you have a little or a lot of hair. If you run, work out and get sweaty, you need it. If you live a normal day, you need it. Even if you did not move all day, your hair would still get greasy and stinky and you need the shampoo. That's your body. It's alive and it hosts bacteria, uses energy and gets rid of waste so, of course, we need toothpaste, soap and shampoo.

Duster: Some are made out of feathers and some out of high tech microfibres. Regardless, a duster removes (or sometimes just moves around) the dust that settles on your things at home. If there were ongoing construction in your house, you would need it for sure. In day to day life, eventually the dust accumulates from people living and moving in the home. But even if you are gone from your house for a month or two and no one is home, when you come back, you will need to dust.

Broom: A broom is another one of those great, genius inventions that just doesn't get the credit it deserves. I'll prove it. Have you ever needed a broom but didn't have one? What do you do? You find something that functions the same as a broom. After a huge party with lots of guests, food and commotion, you need a broom to clean up. Day to day living in a house requires a broom to sweep every day or the floors get dirty and dusty. Even when the house is vacant, in time, you still need a broom for dirt, dust and spiderwebs.

The parable of the householder in Matthew 20:1-6 shows clearly, in a way that hurts, that we are all in the same situation when it comes to God's generosity and grace. We appreciate the bar of soap or toothbrush depending on how badly we need it. Who is forgiven much loves much (Jeremiah 33:8, Ezekiel 37:23).

We cannot go through one day without being affected by our surroundings. Some jump right in and immerse themselves. Some live uneventfully and still get affected by contact with sin and troubles. It is all around us. And still, some set themselves apart from this world to devote to prayer in monasteries or to the ministry or to studies. We can't escape the influence of sin or the problems that arise.

What are God's instruments to remove plaque, dirt and dust from our lives? Forgiveness, grace, compassion, rest, direction, teaching, guidance, love.

How do we know that? It's surprisingly very simple. Read the Bible and pray. I believe that one should begin reading at the beginning of the Bible and not worry about commentaries and amplifications. Choose a readable version and start reading. It's a big book! Get started and read a little everyday,

We all need God's cleansing. Whether you are a new Christian or you've been at it for a while; whether you've read the Bible all your life or you are starting fresh; whether you are in the battle or on the sidelines, talk to God every day!

Prayer

Heavenly Father, I am Yours. I want to do what is right. I fail sometimes. I fail more times than I care to admit. But, as usual, I rely on Your forgiveness and strength to restore and renew. Thanks for being so kind. Thanks for being so patient.

_____

_____

_____

_____

_____

barefoot in the wind

Any fool can count the seeds in an apple.
Only God can count all the apples in one seed.

~ Robert H. Schuller

A man can no more diminish God's glory
by refusing to worship Him than a lunatic
can put out the sun by scribbling the word,
'darkness' on the walls of his cell.

~ C.S. Lewis

How long shall I cry and You will not hear
Or cry to You "violence!" and You will not save

Just look around and you will see
I'm working in you unbelievably
Let all the earth be silent

I'll wait and I'll watch it will not delay
And if I don't understand I'll still obey

As oceans and sees cover the globe
The earth will be filled with the glory of the LORD
Let all the earth sing praise to Him

I love the story of Habakkuk. I love his tenacity and his endurance. I also love that God cared
enough to show him the future in order to answer his concerns about the present. We need to

look at the future that God has already revealed to us through His Word in order to be better able to handle our present situation.

Habakkuk 1

How long, Lord, must I call for help,
    but you do not listen?
Or cry out to you, "Violence!"
    but you do not save?
Why do you make me look at injustice?
    Why do you tolerate wrongdoing?
Destruction and violence are before me;
    there is strife, and conflict abounds.
Therefore the law is paralyzed,
    and justice never prevails.
The wicked hem in the righteous,
    so that justice is perverted.

The Lord's Answer

"Look at the nations and watch—
    and be utterly amazed.
For I am going to do something in your days
    that you would not believe,
    even if you were told.
I am raising up the Babylonians,
    that ruthless and impetuous people,
who sweep across the whole earth
    to seize dwellings not their own.
They are a feared and dreaded people;
    they are a law to themselves
    and promote their own honour.
Their horses are swifter than leopards,
    fiercer than wolves at dusk.
Their cavalry gallops headlong;
    their horsemen come from afar.

They fly like an eagle swooping to devour;
*   they all come intent on violence.*
Their hordes advance like a desert wind
*   and gather prisoners like sand.*
They mock kings
*   and scoff at rulers.*
They laugh at all fortified cities;
*   by building earthen ramps they capture them.*
Then they sweep past like the wind and go on—
*   guilty people, whose own strength is their god."*

Serpent of Healing

I read a story in Numbers 21:5-9 that I thought was strange. God sent snakes to bite people when they were complaining in the wilderness. Then I thought of something. Imagine three or four kids in a car with their parents going on a long trip. What happens as soon as they leave the driveway?

"Are we there yet?" And the parents sigh.

"I'm thirsty." And the parents give them water.

"I'm hungry." And the parents give them food.

"I'm tired." And the parents give them a pillow.

"I'm bored." And the parents give them a game or a toy.

But, if it escalates:

"My stupid parents took me away from playing a great game just to bring us to our stupid relatives. This whole trip is stupid." Well, in the old days, parents would give a good, swift spanking and, voilà, you have respectful kids and a peaceful excursion.

The children of Israel were slaves in Egypt. Crash, bang, boom and ten plagues later they are free. Over half a million of them left Egypt and started walking across the desert on a long trip. But God did not leave them alone. God led them with a cloud by day and a pillar of fire by night. When they were thirsty, they told Moses and Moses prayed and God sent them water out of a rock - - in the desert - - for over half a million people.

When they were hungry, they complained to Moses and Moses prayed. God sent them manna from heaven everyday except Sabbath for over half a million people.

God took care of them. They walked for 40 years and their sandals didn't wear out. It even says in the Bible that their feet didn't hurt. For forty years? In the same shoes? That is a miracle!!!

At this point in the story in Numbers, the complaining has escalated. They are saying, "This is stupid. Why did God bring us out to this stupid desert? We have no water. We have no food. We had food in Egypt. Moses is stupid. God is stupid." Just like the parents in by-gone days spanked their children to get them back on track, God sent serpents to bite the people. But look:

God told Moses to make a serpent out of bronze and put it on a pole and anyone who looked at it would be healed of their snake bite. The people realized that God was taking care of them. God *does* love them. But even with that free and immediate healing opportunity, some people refused to look at the serpent to be healed. Today, some people are like that, too. They don't know that God loves them. They think God is stupid and that believing God is stupid. They think going to church is stupid. Praying is stupid. God doesn't send snakes but He did send Jesus.

In John 3:14 Jesus said, "Just as Moses lifted up the snake in the wilderness so the Son of Man must be lifted up." So all that people have to do is to look at Jesus and acknowledge, God did that for me? He *does* love me.

Prayer

You did all that for me? You *do* love me.

_____

_____

_____

_____

_____

_____

7
barely audible

And above all, watch with glittering eyes the whole world around you because the greatest secrets are always hidden in the most unlikely places.

~ Roald Dahl

The word listen contains the same letters as the word silent.

~ Alfred Brendel

Lyrics

When I saw you this morning
Too timid to greet you
You were standing by a group of friends
The sun was in your eyes
But when I saw you this evening
Apprehension and sorrow
All alone now
Far from home now
Needing a friend
Then I looked in the mirror
And I started to wonder
What have I that I can give to you
To make you change your mind
If I could write you a love song
Slip it into your pocket
Would you hear it
Would you know it
Would you know it was me

The voice that sings to you
Too softly to hear
The song that it brings to you
May easily touch your tear
The liminal calling
Barely audible breath
The cadence falling
It's me I confess

In which order do you say the directions on the compass? How did you learn them? Was there a saying that helped you remember the order? North, south, east, west? West, north, east south? Does it matter in which order we refer to them? Maybe it doesn't matter. Why worry about the details? Often, when reading the Bible, we may skip the minor details and not worry much about the minutiae. Perhaps it's difficult to pronounce the names of carefully-placed geographical locations. Maybe the meticulously-recorded dates and timing are irrelevant to you at this point. But, God wrote the Bible and organized every detail. Every detail is important. Nothing is wasted in God's economy.

If you get bored with the 'begats,' diminish the details and slap over the small, seemingly insignificant segments, that does not preclude their importance. What it means is that you don't yet understand the full significance. An example is the order of the points on the compass.

In Luke 13:29, Jesus states that people will come from the east, west, north and south and sit down in the Kingdom of God. One may say, the particular order is not the point. Jesus meant that people will have their origins from all countries of the earth and will be part of the Kingdom of God in Jerusalem whereas some children of Abraham will be cast out. Interestingly, in Psalm 107:3, God will call them out of all the nations where he scattered them and gather the Jews to return to Jerusalem from all points of the compass in that same order. Now there are many places in the Bible that discuss the compass directions and each seems to mention the four directions in a different order. This particular order, east, west, north and south is interesting as we outline events in history.

Not only is the concept that God will regather Israel true but, even the literal words Jesus spoke are prophetic. History records that in the late 1800's and early 1900's Jews began returning to Jerusalem from Middle Eastern countries such as Syria and Lebanon et cetera. After the Second Word War, there was an influx of Jews from Western Europe. In 1989, Russia opened it's doors under glasnost. When previously, Jews were not allowed to emigrate, now they were free to leave Russia and make their home in Israel. Finally, in 1991, the country of Ethiopia warned Israel that they would kill 14,000 Jews if they did not leave the country. Within 72 hours, Israel flew jumbo jets and evacuated thousands of Jews and relocated them in Israel. They called this *Operation Solomon*.

We often skip over small details in the Bible like personal names, geographical places or the order some things are mentioned. Because God wrote the Bible and not humans, every detail has an eternity of meaning.

John 10:27

My sheep listen to my voice; I know them and they follow me.

Our Little Secret

In the 1920's a newspaper advertised a job as a systems operator in radio communications. It was shortly after World War One, many young men were looking for work. The advertisement told the men to arrive at the Federal Communications Commission office at 9:00am. Our friend, Thomas, was also desperate for a job but he was taking care of his sick mother that morning so he did not arrive in the office of the Federal Communications Commission until almost 11:00.

As he entered, he saw a large waiting room full of young men just like himself. He hesitated. He listened. The men were draped over their chairs, some with head in hands, slouching and leaning over. Someone addressed him, "Come on in and wait like the rest of us. No one has been called yet."

Thomas listened. He sat on a nearby vacant chair with a straight back, hands on his knees, poised like he had heard something. In a few minutes, Thomas walked into the manager's office.

I drive a car. Many people do. The road speaks to me. It tells me where I should go and when. Not the road signs. I'm talking about the road. It sends me messages. It communicates with me. I'll tell you our little secret. It's the lines in the middle of the road that speak to me. They tell me that I can't see the traffic up ahead so I should definitely stay in my lane. They tell me I can pass and cross over the broken line. The lines tell me that others could be passing now. They tell me don't even think about crossing this yellow line. Now that you know the code, it's not a secret anymore.

Our friend, Thomas knew the code, Morse code. When he walked into that office waiting room, he did hear something. He heard clicking. Everyone else heard the clicking, too, but, Thomas knew what it meant. As he listened to the clicking Morse Code, he heard the words spelled out: "Come into the office. If you can understand this, come into the office." So he did and he got the job.

The world is like all those people in that waiting room, waiting, losing hope, getting discouraged. They say, "God isn't speaking to us. God doesn't care about us. God must not exist." Yet, God is speaking. Like that Morse Code, He is communicating but many don't know what they are supposed to be listening to or how to understand what they hear.

Do you know Morse Code? Do you know what's being communicated? You might hear Morse Code but not understand it. I could tell you what the clicking means but how could you be sure what I'm saying is right?

How can you listen to God?

The Bible.

In it you will find what God values, what He wants, who He is, what He is going to do and how you fit into all this.

Prayer

If Your voice is sometimes barely audible, it is my responsibility to quiet down and listen. To quiet down. To quiet down and listen. Please be patient with me and help me to quiet down and listen to Your voice.

_____

_____

_____

_____

_____

_____

8
can't escape

Think you're escaping and run into yourself.
Longest way round is the shortest way home.

~ James Joyce

I love those who love me,
and those who seek me diligently find me.

~ Proverbs 8:17

Anytime you talk to Him He will hear
Anytime you go to Him He will stay
Anytime you walk with Him
He'll always be there
Anytime you cry to Him He will know
Anytime you call to Him He will go
Anytime you wait for Him
He'll always be there

You can soar as high as an eagle
But you can't leave the hand of God
And if you make your home in the stars
You're not higher than His love

You can live in a rock or you can live in a condo
He sees deep in your heart
If you have many friends or it you have only one
He's waiting to talk to you

There's a fire that burns deep in your heart
This desire within you now
Just to reach out your hand to find some other hand
I could show you how

When I read the words from the book of Obadiah, I infer anger and vengeance toward a proud and rebellious group. The context leads to that interpretation. Yet, even stretched out of context, the words hold true. Whether one is in opposition to God or one is searching or one is willingly surrendered, God's message is the same because His plan is the same for all people.

Obadiah v 3,4

The pride of your heart has deceived you, you who live in the clefts of the rocks and make your home on the heights, you who say to yourself, 'Who can bring me down to the ground?' Though you soar like the eagle and make your nest among the stars, from there I will bring you down," declares the Lord.

Beyond God's Reach

Chapter forty is the beginning of the second half of the book of Isaiah. You can see a difference between the two halves. The first thirty-nine chapters focus on Judah's sin, coming judgement and approaching destruction. From chapters forty to sixty-six, the focus is on forgiveness, restoration, God's plan for the Messiah's reign and God living among us on earth. Chapter forty begins with news of comfort. Isaiah was told to give the message that said, "Take comfort. Your sins are forgiven. Your warfare has ended." Good news for sure.

Two chapters before that, Hezekiah was sick (Isaiah 38:1). The lab test results showed that he was going to die. Maybe it was cancer, something slow and inevitable. Hezekiah prayed. He had done all the things God had asked of him. He had been loyal. He loved God. He was sad to have to die with so many things left undone. Plus, he didn't have an heir to the throne. Miraculously, Hezekiah was given fifteen more years by God and in that time, he had a son, Manasseh.

Manasseh began to rule as king when he was twelve years old because Hezekiah's appointed time was up. Of all the kings of Judah, Manasseh ruled the longest: fifty-five years on the throne. With such good role models as Hezekiah and Isaiah, Manasseh should have left a better legacy than that of being the most evil king in Judah's history.

He worshiped the stars; he worshiped false gods; he set up idols of every kind. He sacrificed his children to heathen gods. He practised witchcraft and black magic and Satanic worship. Manasseh even had Isaiah killed when he gave orders to murder the prophets and priests of Yahweh. It's easy to conclude that it might have been better if Hezekiah, Manasseh's father, had died before the fifteen years of grace. Where was God's hand in these events? Where was God? Did He lose track of these people? Didn't he care what happened?

To make a long story short, Manasseh was taken by the Babylonians. They put hooks in his face and his chest and walked him for hundreds of miles across the desert to Babylon and threw him into a dungeon to rot.

While rotting, Manasseh re-thought his whole life. He came to his senses and realized that he had been wrong. He asked God to forgive him. Would God forgive all this evil? God forgave him and restored him to his throne in Jerusalem. That is unheard of!! How does that happen? God must have had His hand in these events.

There were a few more kings before Babylon totally destroyed the nation of Judah, as Isaiah had foretold. It took about 120 years for his prophecies of devastation to be fulfilled and 700 more years for his prophecies about Jesus' birth and ministry.

From chapter forty on, Isaiah writes about restoration: first the suffering servant by whose stripes we are healed, who was wounded for our transgressions. Then the conquering Saviour who will again come to us and set up God's kingdom, His holy mountain, where no one will hurt or destroy and we will live in peace and righteousness.

All the time Isaiah wrote, things were bad and they were about to get worse. In our time, things are bad and they are continually getting worse: our lives, our laws, our liberties are all spiralling out of control. But God's message today is the same message that he gave to Isaiah 2700 years ago.

Be comforted. You are not unreachable. You could be the most evil king in all of Judah's history and still not be beyond God's reach.

Prayer

People and all the evil they do are like the grass that withers. Meaningless. Powerless. In You only can I find the forgiveness and the restoration I am looking for. Thank You for reaching out and for finding me with Your love and compassion.

_____

_____

_____

_____

_____

9

darkness into light

> I saw that the most important thing I had to do was to give myself to the reading of the Word of God and to meditation of it.
>
> ~ George Mueller

> Darkness cannot drive out darkness: only light can do that. Hate cannot drive out hate: only love can do that.
>
> ~ Martin Luther King Jr.

I know that I have lingered far too long by the still and restful waters
I opened my mouth without a song when I try it seems so wrong
I have remained still
I have restrained myself
The rage inside of me
But the light slips through my fingers
Til there's nothing
Nothing left to see

I will lead the blind
In a way they have not known
With eyes that see
I will call them mine
Making them my own
You belong to me
I will turn all this darkness
Into light

Sometimes when I'm weary I need someone to carry me
I'm out of words and out of breath and I break so easily

I have a fear
My eyes will close
Without You near
Then I always hear your voice
I strain to listen
And I hear You say

My generation had the task of toppling the status quo: deconstructing traditional ideas and practices. I must admit, I was trained well in the field of education and, for a while, became what I was being molded to become. I'm talking about social activism and rethinking our classrooms, what we teach and how. It was new and exciting when it involved deconstructing *Goldilocks and the Three Bears* in a social context. However, like the 1958 creature classic, *The Blob*, it began to spread out and take over aspects outside of education. For me, religion was important and therefore, it, too, became subjected to the deconstruction process.

The antidote to such brainwashing is this: God is real. He is a real person. He loves people on this earth and He has a plan for us. We can participate in that plan if we want. The only way to combat the powers that vie for our attention is to get to know the God of Abraham, Isaac and Jacob who told us from the beginning what He is doing. It is the same story echoing throughout the Bible and throughout history.

Isaiah 42:16

I will lead the blind by ways that have not known, along unfamiliar paths I will guide them; I will turn the darkness into light before them and make the rough places smooth. These are the things I will do; I will not forsake them.

Light Source

Our main natural source of light on this planet is the sun. The moon is a reflection of the original light. We can make fire and get light from fire, harness and use it. There are transient flashes of lightning in an electrical storm and, of course, electricity lights up the world. The Northern lights are wispy fingers of the sun wriggling on the edges of the orb and fireflies are little tickles of light. All in all, we are in perpetual darkness until and unless a light source imposes on that darkness.

The two disciples on the road to Emmaus had lived in the light and were now in complete darkness. This is my observation about most Christians I have known, including me! We read the Bible but, still we are blind. We talk to God but, still we are deaf.

Those two disciples walked with Jesus for perhaps seven miles without recognizing him. They were devastated after Jesus' crucifixion. They should have been elated to witness the events that Jesus foretold, notwithstanding the brutality and the suffering. In Luke 24:25, we read that Jesus called them fools. He rebuked them not because they were sad or frustrated or had an emotional response to the events they had just witnessed. He rebuked them because they did not apply the scripture that they knew. But, don't worry, he didn't stop there. By going through and explaining scripture, he unveiled that the events of that weekend had already been spoken of by the prophets and by Jesus himself.

Once they had arrived at their destination, the two disciples invited Jesus in for the meal. Jesus was definitely a guest in this home. According to Jewish tradition, it was the host who blessed the bread. By what was known as the Messianic Rule, it was understood that no one should stretch out his hand to bless the bread before the Messiah. The authority to bless the bread clearly belonged to the host or the Messiah. When Jesus the stranger acted as the one who had authority to break the bread and bless it before the meal, he was proclaiming that he is the Messiah. By this act, their eyes were instantly opened and ironically, Jesus disappeared.

If we, in the same position as those two disciples, are responding with fear, anxiety, frustration, confusion and anger to current events, then we need to know Scripture better. We can no longer afford to be lax. It is now urgent! Christians need to be equipped with the knowledge of Scripture so that when these things that have been foretold actually happen, our response will be to raise up our heads for we recognize that our redemption is near (Luke 21:28).

Prayer

Thank You that we who walk in darkness can see Your light and reflect that light to others.

_____

_____

_____

_____

_____

10

daughters of jerusalem

He who touches Israel touches the apple of my eye.

~ Zechariah 2:8

However, the days are coming, declares the Lord, when it will no longer be said, As surely as the Lord lives, who brought the Israelites up out of Egypt'

~ Jeremiah 16:14

Lyrics

Daughters of Jerusalem
Celebrate your joy
Daughters of Jerusalem
Sing His praise

Tell the Holy City
Do not be afraid
God is in the midst of you
He will make His home in you

Sing out loud to Zion
Do not be dismayed
God is your strong presence
He will calm you in His love

Do not be disheartened
God will bring you home
He will heal your brokenness
He will gladly sing for you

Sing for you
Sing for you
Sing for you
Sing for you

Whereas a nation has been scattered and oppressed for thousands of years, those thousands of years carried a promise of regathering, restoring and reviving. "Next year in Jerusalem." They may have seen themselves as cursed and forgotten but, they are blessed and remembered. Why would a scattered people continue to remember feasts and celebrate harvests they did not gather? Why would they continue to act out rituals layered in meaning that they would not understand until years later? Because God, who is real and who keeps His word, planned it all out and told us from the beginning what would happen so that when it does happen, we would know beyond a shadow of a doubt that He is who He said He is.

If the past has unfolded as God said it would then, we can be confident that the future will also be as God has said. So, tell Jerusalem! Give Jerusalem the message! Celebrate! God will do as He said.

Zephaniah 3:14 -20

Sing, Daughter Zion; shout aloud, Israel! Be glad and rejoice with all your heart, Daughter Jerusalem! The Lord has taken away your punishment, he has turned back your enemy. The Lord, the King of Israel, is with you; never again will you fear any harm.

On that day they will say to Jerusalem, "Do not fear, Zion; do not let your hands hang limp. The Lord your God is with you, the Mighty Warrior who saves. He will take great delight in you; in his love he will no longer rebuke you, but will rejoice over you with singing." "I will remove from you all who mourn over the loss of your appointed festivals, which is a burden and reproach for you.

At that time I will deal with all who oppressed you. I will rescue the lame; I will gather the exiles. I will give them praise and honor in every land where they have suffered shame. At that time I will gather you; at that time I will bring you home. I will give you honor and praise among all the peoples of the earth when I restore your fortunes before your very eyes," says the Lord.

Party

In our church, we have a table in the sanctuary covered by a cloth embroidered with the words "Holiness Unto The Lord" across the front. It holds a Bible and it is situated in front of the mercy seat which is a place where people can kneel and pray.

With a cloth that says, 'Holiness Unto the Lord,' the table, one would think, would be a reminder that nothing is holy except God. Not people, not ideas, not things, not the holiness table. Years of calling it the "holiness" table seems to have rendered the table itself holy. There is a rule at our church that nothing superfluous should be haphazardly placed on the Holiness Table. I get it. That "holiness table" is a symbol. It represents something. Here is another symbol.

One day, I had the responsibility of telling the children's story and I brought bags of chips and popcorn and pretzels to the front and placed them on the holiness table.

Those things aren't really food. We don't eat them for breakfast, they aren't lunch food and we don't cook with them to make supper. Those bags of snacks are really party food, aren't they? They can be considered party food or fun food. I might have shocked a few old souls by where I placed those bags of party food but, I wanted to relate to a time when Jesus did sort of the same thing.

Jesus was invited to a wedding feast in Cana. He was minding his own business when his mom came to him, tapped him on the shoulder and said something like, "Pssst. We are out of wine."

Jesus reminded her that it wasn't yet his time to start doing miracles. His mother knew him well and told the servers to do whatever Jesus told them to do. Jesus accepted the responsibility usually reserved for the bridegroom and looked around. He saw jugs of holy water that their religion used to ceremonially wash themselves as a symbol of cleanliness or holiness.

At a first-century Jewish wedding, it was the responsibility of the bridegroom to provide the wine. This explains why, after tasting the water-made-wine, the steward came directly to the groom with his puzzled observation: "Everyone brings out the choice wine first and then the cheaper wine after the guests have had too much to drink; but you have saved the best till now" (John 2:10).

In changing water into wine, Jesus was in fact acting as the definitive bridegroom, fulfilling the prophecy of Isaiah that Yahweh would indeed come to marry his people. Moreover, in providing 180 gallons (the excessive amount that John's Gospel reports in John 2:6), he was hinting at Isaiah's expectation (Isaiah 55:13) and Joel's prediction (Joel 3:18) that the hills themselves would run with wine. Jesus used these holy jugs filled with holy water and told the servants to serve the guests out of those jugs. They obeyed and wine came out: the best wine anyone had ever tasted.

Jesus took something that was a symbol of religion (the jugs) and turned it into a symbol of a relationship with God (a party). He used a symbol of a party to describe our relationship with God. When the lost coin was found, the woman had a party! When the lost sheep was found, the shepherd had a party. When the prodigal son returned, the father had a party (Luke 15). Jesus said the kingdom of heaven is like a rich man who threw a party (Matthew 22:2).

Maybe your church has something like our holiness table that reminds you of how sacred and holy your religion is. Remember that instead of the religion and its rules, God wants to have a relationship with you and being in a relationship with Him is like, well, a party!!!

Prayer

Lord, remind me daily that You keep Your promises. Your word goes from Your mouth and does not return to You empty. You accomplish what You set out to do. In addition, You love us so much that You celebrate when we return to You!! A relationship with You is like a party! Help me to find Your rejoicing over me enough reason for me to rejoice!!

_____

_____

_____

_____

_____

11

everybody but the bride

If you think something is missing in your life, it is probably YOU.

~ Robert Holden

How did it get so late so soon?

~ Dr. Seuss

They all arrived
They all brought lamps
Prepared for the long night ahead
It would've been fine
If it happened on time
They would be happily wed

These things happen
You know how it goes
Someone is inevitably late
There's no one to blame
They all fell asleep
It was just too long a wait

The announcement was made
The arrival announced
It was a shocking surprise
To awake in the dark and be
Easily bounced
From the group that began to rise

These things happen, you know
You know how it goes
Someone is inevitably late
There's no one to blame
They all fell asleep
It was just too long a wait

Go and get your own oil
We haven't got enough
We simply can't share from our store
He'll think we're all fools
He'll throw us all out
We can't take the chance
You're on your own

These things happen all the time
You know how it goes
Someone is inevitably late
There's no one to blame
They all fell asleep
It was just too long a wait

To make the best of a situation
They left to refill
The oil that diminished overnight
When the party began
They saw it and ran
But the heavy door was closing in their sight

These things happen
You know how it goes
Someone is inevitably late
There's no one to blame
They all fell asleep
It was just too long a wait

Everybody but the bride
They didn't get to go inside
Like a puzzle
The missing piece
Late is late even if you wait
They didn't get to go inside

In the parable about the ten virgins (Matthew 12:5), Jesus mentioned everyone who had a role in the wedding feast except the bride herself. This is significant because some say we who are waiting for Christ's return are the virgins with our lamps trimmed and burning with abundant oil supply. The oil is the Spirit, the groom is Jesus. There is ample evidence in the Scriptures that the Bride of Christ is the church. So, who exactly are the ten virgins? And more specifically, let's differentiate between who are the five who had oil (but wouldn't share) and the five who did not have oil, attempted to renew their supply but were, unfortunately, too late.

Matthew 25

"At that time the kingdom of heaven will be like ten virgins who took their lamps and went out to meet the bridegroom. Five of them were foolish and five were wise. The foolish ones took their lamps but did not take any oil with them. The wise ones, however, took oil in jars along with their lamps. The bridegroom was a long time in coming, and they all became drowsy and fell asleep. "At midnight the cry rang out: 'Here's the bridegroom! Come out to meet him!' "Then all the virgins woke up and trimmed their lamps. The foolish ones said to the wise, 'Give us some of your oil; our lamps are going out.' "'No,' they replied, 'there may not be enough for both us and you. Instead, go to those who sell oil and buy some for yourselves.'

"But while they were on their way to buy the oil, the bridegroom arrived. The virgins who were ready went in with him to the wedding banquet. And the door was shut.

"Later the others also came. 'Lord, Lord,' they said, 'open the door for us!'

"But he replied, 'Truly I tell you, I don't know you.'

"Therefore keep watch, because you do not know the day or the hour.

Jewish Wedding

These girls all showed up. They all brought lamps. They were responsible and committed and focused on why they were there. Still, what a story! Not only is it from the girls' perspective but, we don't even get a glimpse of the bride. Every character in the story is mentioned, everybody but the bride. Some brought extra oil. Some did not. They all fell asleep. The groom announced his coming but the bride was absent. Why? What does that mean? Who is the bride? What is the oil? Who is the bridegroom? To understand this parable better, we need an explanation of the traditional Jewish wedding.

In the Old Testament, marriage is the supreme metaphor to express the faithful, life-giving and intense love of God for the world. For example, Isaiah, with audacity that makes you gasp, says to the people Israel, "Your builder (God) wants to marry you." We've heard about obeying God and seeking God and trying to please God but the Bible uniquely presents Jehovah God as seeking us even to the point of wanting to marry us; to pour out His love for us without restriction.

Isaiah (25:6) continues to say that when the Messiah comes, he will preside at a great wedding banquet at which "juicy meats and pure, choice wine" will be served. Indeed, he tells us, there will be drink in such abundance that "the very hills will run with wine."

So, now that we identify who the bridegroom is (Jesus), let's look at the traditional Jewish customs of courtship and marriage to better understand what analogy Jesus was making when he said he is the bridegroom.

There are seven steps in the Jewish matrimonial customs. The first step in the Jewish wedding system was the Shiddukhin (the arrangement or the making of the match). The father of the bride usually took the initial steps by approving the girl who would be the best match for his son. This step could be done at any time: either when the two were young children or later when a son chose a girl for himself. The father might also assign the task to a trusted servant.

The Shiddukhin that our Heavenly Father has made for us is found in John 3:16: "For God so loved the world that He gave His one and only son that whoever believes in him should not perish but have everlasting life." Our Heavenly Father has already followed through on the first step by making the necessary arrangements.

The second step is the giving of gifts accompanied by a promise from the groom. The father of the groom transfers the bride price and a gift from the groom to the father of the bride. The gift is called a Mohar. This gift was like a blood-covenant between the two parties involved. A marriage represented bringing together two families and cemented their relationship forever. One family gave away a beloved daughter and the other family compensated by giving a very valuable gift. The gift from the bridegroom was called the Mattan. This gift was to represent the enormous love the groom held for his bride-to-be.

The final gift, called the Shiluhim, was given by the father of the bride to his daughter as a portion of her inheritance. Specifically, it helped the daughter prepare for the wedding. Traditionally, the sons would inherit the father's wealth and the daughter would leave the father's estate and live with her husband. The father's money, here, went to the daughter for wedding preparations.

Everyone involved with this step gave gifts *except the bride.* She was the reason for the marriage. She was the object of love. Neither does anyone have to give gifts to Jesus for him to love us. We simply have to do what the Jewish Bride would do in the next step.

The third step was called the Ketubah. Jewish marriages were legalized with a written marriage contract. In this contract, a Jewish husband was responsible for all of the wife's medical needs, the support of her daughters, an inheritance for the sons and a respectable funeral and resting place for her.

After finishing the written contract, the groom promised to return for the bride once he finished building a place for the two of them to live. The bridegroom, after signing the Ketubah, presented two cups of wine. He drank the first cup, an act to depict his love for the girl. The second cup remained on the table while the bridegroom prayed.

At this point the bride chose to drink from the second cup or leave it on the table. By drinking the wine from the cup, she accepted the bridegroom. By letting it sit, she rejected the Ketubah. Once the bride drank from the cup, the Ketubah was sealed and the young couple were known to be betrothed.

Step five. The betrothal or Kiddushin is different from what we know as the engagement period. For one year, a Jewish man is exempt from military service for the purpose of building a bridal chamber. In John 14:1-3 we find Jesus saying, "Do not let your hearts be troubled. You believe in God; believe also in me. My Father's house has many rooms; if that were not so, would I have told you that I am going there to prepare a place for you? And if I go and prepare a place for you, I will come back and take you to be with me that you also may be where I am." That's the analogy he was making! He is the bridegroom. He has fulfilled these things.

The bride used the year betrothal time for preparation. She always wore a veil out in public to show that she was set apart to marry her bridegroom. She was purchased with a bride price and everyone knew she was consecrated to another. The Hebrew word for the consecrated bride is Kudeshet meaning one who is betrothed, sanctified or dedicated to another. The young Kudeshet lived in anticipation of the return of her groom. She never knew for sure when the groom might appear so she kept a constant vigil. She routinely kept an oil lamp lit in a visible place every night. The bridegroom would sneak out to see if the bride was burning the midnight oil in his honour.

The betrothal period gave each party time to reflect on their relationship. The groom prepared the best environment for his bride. The bride presented herself without any stain of unholiness on her wedding day. The parallel becomes clearer. We are the bride. Christ is the bridegroom.

The next step, step six, in the Jewish wedding custom is called the Nessuin, or the nuptials (wedding). When the father of the groom decided that the bridal chamber was in perfect condition, he would announce that it was time for the groom to redeem his bride. Finally, with great joy, the groom and his friends made plans to return to his bride. This was his moment! He paraded to the bride's house arriving at midnight. The shofar (trumpet) announced his arrival!!!

Upon arrival, the groom's party would not enter the house. Rather, on the groom's signal, the best friend of the groom would blast the shofar, then they would all call out, 'The bridegroom is here. Come out to meet him.'

Step seven. Arriving at the father's estate, the young couple would be treated like royalty. They would be greeted by the family and then retire to a specially prepared place called the Huppah, or canopy, which symbolized that the bride was now under the groom's protection. There they would spend an entire week alone where all the provisions they would need were already stored.

Meanwhile, the father hosted a feast for the entire week, while his guests waited for the the bride and groom to return for yet another celebration to finalize the marriage. After this week of celebration, the new bride would remain inside the Huppah for another seven days hidden from view until she was ready to begin her new role.

Our God is a God who pays meticulous attention to detail. He fulfills what He has established. He paid a high price to secure a bride for His son. He will not fail to send His son back to reclaim his beloved.

It was on the cross that Jesus drank the cup of acceptance to his Bride. He finished his Siddukhin mission. He signed the Ketubah with his own blood and imparted the free gifts (Mohar and Mattan) of salvation and eternal life to his betrothed. Jesus has already started his mission to construct a huppah for his bride. Soon, when his Father judges that all is complete, He will release Jesus to return for his bride.

Those of us who are the bride of Christ await the shofar blast. When that trumpet sounds, in the twinkling of an eye, we will be ready to meet our bridegroom, Jesus. And in the words of Revelation 19:7, "Let us rejoice and be glad and give him glory! For the wedding of the Lamb has come, and his bride has made herself ready."

Prayer

Father in heaven, we scarcely know how to respond to such love. You have shown us over and over how much You love us yet, it's difficult to take it all in.

We have heard this all our lives that You love us, that You *are* love. Here, we have heard it again with the analogy of the bride and groom. Please make this a reality foremost in our minds and hearts.

Father, thank You for sending Jesus. Thank You that, as we see history unfolding, it will soon be time to send him again. We look forward to that day. Keep our hearts softened in love and compassion for others. Help us to prepare ourselves to see you soon.

We do love you, Jesus and we want to be ready to welcome you when you return.

12
gettin' down hope

Hope is being able to see that there is light despite all of the darkness.
~ Desmond Tutu

We must accept finite disappointment but never lose infinite hope.
~ Martin Luther King Jr.

I got hope
When others are gettin' down
I got hope
I'm gonna turn myself around
Jesus has given me the love I need
And in him I can claim victory
I got hope

They're screamin' 'bout our air
They're screamin' 'bout our trees
They're still choppin' 'em down doin' as they please
But this ol' world
Is on her last breath
This hope that I know
Goes far beyond death
I got hope

You say the old man
Suckin' up your last dime
The kids know your name
But you don't have the time

Your pockets are empty
Your knees gettin' thin
This hope that I know
Sure gonna win
I got hope

Well my man
Kicked me out of the house
He threw out my best shirt and
Called me a louse
But I know I'm saved
And I know I'm loved
This hope that I know
Comes from above
I got hope

The one thing we need in or world today is hope. Choose a common ailment and its antidote is hope. Hope can get you through the worst situations. One caveat: what you hope in must be real. False hope may get you over some obstacle at the time but, the later discovery of its falsehood will obliterate the good that may have come from it. Deception is devastating.

1 Peter 1:3

Praise be to the God and Father of our Lord Jesus Christ! In his great mercy he has given us new birth into a living hope through the resurrection of Jesus Christ from the dead.

How did They Miss It?

God declared to Adam and Eve his plan of redemption in the garden of Eden. The Jewish priests and people were constantly asking God for a sign when He would send the Messiah. God answered their prayer with a very precise prophecy telling them when the Messiah would come to Israel. Yet they missed it! However, there was a group of men who were watching for this prophecy and waiting for it to be fulfilled. Who were they?

The three wise men. Whether they were three or not, we do not know. Because three gifts are mentioned, we surmise that there was one person to a gift. For our purposes, let's use the three wise men of Christmas to represent the magi group.

How did they know that the star they saw was so special that they would set out on a very long journey on camels to give presents to the coming King? Wait a minute. Who told them about the king? They weren't even Jews. They were pagan.

Over 600 years before Jesus was born, God revealed this precious secret to Daniel. Daniel was taken to Babylon. He was a high official in the royal Babylonian government. He prayed to God every day and studied the Scriptures. When he refused to pray to the king (Darius), he was thrown into the lions' den and God kept him safe. In fact, the Magi or wise men in the kingdom had always held Daniel in high regard because Daniel had saved their lives. When had he done that?

Earlier in Daniel's career, the king (Nebuchadnezzar) had a dream he couldn't remember (or chose not to reveal). He was going to kill all the wise men if someone didn't tell him what he had dreamed. It may have been a test to determine the integrity of their positions as "wisemen." Daniel knew that only God could answer the king's request so he prayed and God revealed the dream to Daniel. Because of that, the king spared the lives of Daniel and all the magi.

In those days, there were no printing presses. Only high officials and religious leaders had access to books and written records. The magi were scholars and had access to books. They knew all of Daniel's writing. They had copies of his book and they knew Daniel's prophecy (Daniel 9:24 -27); they counted the years and knew when it was time to be fulfilled. The prophecy was given in detail 600 years before Jesus was born!

So the question is, if these wise men, generations after Daniel's prophecy, who were pagan worshippers of idols, knew and understood the prophecy of the Messiah, why did the Jews miss it? They had Daniel's writings, too. The prophecies were about them.

Long before Jesus was born, Jewish leaders had stopped believing that the Bible was the inspired, sacred word of God. They stopped taking the Bible literally. They thought, maybe God didn't really mean what He said. He must have meant something else. So, they stopped teaching the Bible and the prophecies. (This reminds me of what Satan told Eve in the garden of Eden. When God said, don't eat of the tree or you will die, Satan reassured Eve that God didn't mean what He said). The leaders stopped teaching the Bible. They weren't aware of the prophecies declaring his coming just as the average person today isn't aware of the over 300 prophecies that talk about the second coming of Jesus. They weren't aware of the prophecies so, they missed it.

In Matthew 24:23, Jesus said that we will be able to know when his second coming is close when we read about it in the Bible. In Mark 13:37, Jesus said, "What I say to you, I say to everyone: 'Watch!'" Pay attention: be cautious, be alert and watch!

God is precise concerning the fulfillment of all His prophecies. Not one of His prophecies will fail. The longer you go to school, the more you will hear that God didn't write the Bible and He didn't really mean what He said. We need to be aware of prophecies about the second coming of Jesus so we will not be surprised when they are fulfilled. How do we do that? By reading the Bible. Read it to someone or have someone read it to you then, two people will be hearing the Word of God.

Prayer

Father, You are not a man that You should lie or a son of man that You would change Your mind (Num 23:19). So, when You say over and over that You have plans for us and that You have prepared a place for us, we know that it is true and Your word can be trusted. When You say You are with us and will never leave us, we believe you. When You tell us not to be afraid of the things that happen, we will listen to You. Our hope is in You.

_____

_____

_____

_____

_____

_____

13

going my way

> I am an historian, I am not a believer but, I must confess as a historian
> that this penniless preacher from Nazareth is irrevocably the centre of
> history. Jesus Christ is easily the most dominant figure in all of history.
>
> ~ H.G. Wells

> One road leads home and a thousand roads lead into the wilderness.
>
> ~ C.S. Lewis

When you find me beside those whose
Knees are unbended
You'll find me with nothing to say
When you find me behind those whose paths are unended
You'll know that you're going my way

If you find yourself seeking
An alternate ending or
Turning your eyes to the sea
If you find yourself wishing that
You weren't pretending
You'll know that you're going to be

Going my way
Going my way
If you're knowing the truth and you're
Living the life and you'll
Know that you're going my way

If you've ever imagined
The dream that you're living could
Finish up costing you more
If you ever imagined the shipwreck commotion
Could possibly drift to the shore
If you've ever relinquished a moment of silence
To tighten your grip on a star
If you've ever believed there's a closure to violence
You'll know that you certainly are
Going my way

When you find that you've entered
A tunnel of forgiveness and
Hurled all your wounds to the sky
When you finally realize the pain of perfection
You'll shout the you understand why

When you find me beside those whose
Knees are unbended
You'll find me with nothing to say
When you find me behind those whose paths are unended
You'll know that you're going my way

I find the gospels fascinating. Jesus was fascinating, even from a secular perspective. Historians have determined that he has had the greatest impact on human history. There is no man who has had a greater impact. There is a reason. God is proclaiming His message to the world. Before the 1990's, God and the Bible were a part of our cultural capital. So much so that literary critic Northrop Frye advised that if one wanted to understand the literature of our civilization, one needed to be well-versed in the literature of the Bible. Since the turn of the new century, God and the Bible have been obliterated from the public domain. Rarely is any word heard of them without apology, condescension or accusation.

Thankfully, Jesus Christ is still used abundantly as a swear word keeping his name in the forefront of our common vernacular. (!) Perhaps, even in that context, God can create an opportunity for someone to find a gem of His love.

John 14:6

Jesus answered, "I am the way the truth and the life. No one comes to the Father except through me."

Jesus Went

Jesus went through all the towns and villages, teaching in their synagogues, proclaiming the good news of the kingdom and healing every disease and sickness. When he saw the crowds, he had compassion on them, because they were harassed and helpless, like sheep without a shepherd. Then he said to his disciples, "The harvest is plentiful but the workers are few. Ask the Lord of the harvest, therefore, to send out workers into his harvest" (Matthew 9:35-37).

Jesus went: That's our mandate, isn't it? Go ye therefore and teach all nations . . . from Matthew 28.

Jesus went about: Where did he go? He went around the cities and villages in his area. He went around his circles of influence. He didn't stay put. What are our circles of influence? At home: Maybe you live in an apartment building. There are people everywhere! Do you live in a neighbourhood? Go for a walk. Talk to your neighbours. It is good for your health and it might change their eternal destiny!

Work: Maybe you commute to work. Good for you. Spread out. We need to spread the love of Christ far and near. Wherever you are, whatever you do, do it in love and God will prepare the way for you.

Jesus went about teaching: Did you learn something today? Tell somebody. Maybe you read a verse in the Bible today? Share it. Did God answer your prayer? Tell someone. Maybe you saw a flower or a sunset and started thinking about God's majesty and creation? Share your ideas. Teach people what you know. You may think you are the one in the room who knows the least, but if you know Jesus, you know enough to talk to someone. Tell them your experience. Tell them what God has done for you.

Jesus went about teaching and proclaiming the good news of the kingdom. Do you know what that is? Do you know what he was proclaiming? God's love for us. God's plan for our world. Remember Nebuchadnezzar's dream? The statue with the golden head, the silver breast and arms, the brass torso, the iron legs and the feet of clay and iron that could not stay together? And finally, the rock not cut with hands that comes and knocks the statue down, creating a mountain.

All the kingdoms of the world will crumble. Who has the right to rule? Jesus the Lamb that was slain will topple the kingdoms of men and rule on David's throne forever. We have been invited to share in that beautiful kingdom of peace where wrongs will be righted and God will put His law in our hearts.

"This is the covenant I will make with the people of Israel after that time," declares the Lord. "I will put my law in their minds and write it on their hearts. I will be their God, and they will be my people. No longer will they teach their neighbor, or say to one another, 'Know the Lord,' because they will all know me, from the least of them to the greatest," declares the Lord. "For I will forgive their wickedness and will remember their sins no more" (Jeremiah 31:32-34). That's the kingdom of God that Jesus proclaimed.

He cured every disease and every sickness: I cannot cure diseases and sickness. But I can cure loneliness *and so can you* by sitting with someone and talking to people who have been forgotten. Phone someone to see how they are doing. Visit the elderly who do not get out. Maybe we can't cure diseases but we can give hope in sickness. Maybe we can't heal broken bones but we can tell people the good news about God who can heal brokenness and despair.

What else did Jesus do?

He saw the crowds: I admit, I pass people everyday and I do not see them. I don't know their story, I don't know that they are sick and sad and lost. Jesus saw them. they did not go unnoticed.

He had compassion: Care about people. Don't harden you heart. It might soon be your turn to be in need. Compassion grows out of really listening. The result is a relationship.

Jesus had compassion because *he realized they were like sheep without a shepherd.* Sheep without a shepherd are lost, confused, scared, helpless, afraid, tense, stressed out, depressed, overloaded. That is an accurate description of our society today.

And *he said to his disciples:* He spoke. He spoke in Genesis and the world came into being. He spoke in Mark 4:39 and calmed the sea. He speaks life and love and peace. When he speaks to us, we are enlivened, invigorated and strengthened.

What did he say? *The harvest is plentiful and the labourers are few.* It is an observation. We need to open our eyes to see the state of affairs in our world, our country, our city, our families, our lives.

Therefore ask: We are to ask, to plead, to interact with God not to sit back and observe or to enjoy the wealth and prosperity that we have amassed. If you have wealth, share it; use it. If you have a table, fill it. Share your food. If you have books, lend them or read to someone. If you have time, spend it on others. Whatever you have, use it for God's purposes.

Ask the Lord of the Harvest to send out labourers: Pray that the work gets done. This does not mean that I get to stay home and pray that God sends someone else. It means that God will answer that prayer and send me and send you and send us!!! He already has sent us. If you are breathing, God will use you. Even if you are not, that is no excuse. God used Lazarus when he was dead!!!

Let's not forget the last two words: *His harvest*. After all, this is God's plan, His harvest, His crop, His thing. He set it in motion in Genesis 1. His word will not come back empty. He will do all He said He will do. "As the rain and the snow come down from heaven and do not return to it without watering the earth and making it bud and flourish, so that it yields seed for the sower and bread for the eater, so is my word that goes out from my mouth: It will not return to me empty, but will accomplish what I desire and achieve the purpose for which I sent it" (Isaiah 55:10-11). It is *His harvest*, yet, He invites us to be a part of it.

Prayer

That's awesome. Thank you God for the privilege and the opportunity to be labourers in Your harvest.

_____

_____

_____

_____

_____

_____

14

He feeds His flock

For he hears the lamb's innocent call
And he hears the ewe's tender reply
He is watchful while they are in peace
For they know that their Shepherd is nigh

~ William Blake

God has, in fact, thought of us from eternity
and has loved us as unique individuals. He
has called every one of us by name, as the
Good Shepherd calls His sheep by name.

~ Pope John Paul II

He feeds His flock like a shepherd
Holds the lambs in His arms
He's my rock
He's my friend

If you're lost, God will find you
If you've strayed He'll bring you back
If you're weak He is strong
If you're down He'll pick you up
If you're hurt He will bind you
And make you walk, make you walk

I was lost now I'm found
I was weak now I'm strong
I was blind now I see clearly
All alone now I belong

I was wrong didn't know
God led the way, led the way

The Bible is replete with the metaphor of a kind, compassionate and caring shepherd. That is a message God wants to communicate to us. And that is how we can relate to Him.

Ezekiel 34: 11-16

For this is what the Sovereign LORD says: I myself will search for my sheep and look after them. As a shepherd looks after his scattered flock when he is with them, so will I look after my sheep. I will rescue them from all the places where they were scattered on a day of clouds and darkness.

I will bring them out from the nations and gather them from the countries, and I will bring them into their own land. I will pasture them on the mountains of Israel, in the ravines and in all the settlements in the land. I will tend them in a good pasture, and the mountain heights of Israel will be their grazing land.

There they will lie down in good grazing land, and there they will feed in a rich pasture on the mountains of Israel. I myself will tend my sheep and have them lie down, declares the Sovereign Lord. I will search for the lost and bring back the strays. I will bind up the injured and strengthen the weak, but the sleek and the strong I will destroy. I will shepherd the flock with justice.

All the Answers

Many people are having problems with money these days. Jobs are lost due to changes in the world's economy and upheaval in social structure. That means fathers with no jobs, mothers with no jobs, families with little money, kids without enough food and clothing. People are looking for help. There is no shortage of experts telling you what to do. Based on the covers of magazines week after week, we learn what this world is obsessed with: food, clothes. body image, marriage, going in and out of relationships.

God, however, has all the answers. And this is not a surprise. The One who thought of us and made us also knows how to manage us. His answers are the truth. They are answers that will work. They are not found in popular magazines. They are in the Bible. When we read the Bible, we discover who God is and what He wants for our lives.

Let's not be foolish. When you read of bashing babies' heads against the rocks (Psalm 137) or Jael driving a tent peg through Sisero's head (Judges 4:21), these are not directives from God. If after reading the entire Bible multiple times, you conclude that God is vengeful and powerful, then act accordingly. Make that your starting point for getting to know Him and discard the arrogance that propels you against Him. Read Matthew 25 all the way to verses 26 and 27 to understand that some things just are the way they are, like gravity; you can fight against them but there is no arguing about them.

Jesus said, don't worry about what you will eat or what you will wear. Search for the things of God and all these things will fall into place. Pay attention. If God promised to take care of us so we don't have to worry about our next meal, we are free to worship him and to help others. If we know where our blessings come from, and we know that they come from God, we won't be afraid or stingy or reluctant to help someone in need.

Here is my version of what the psalmist is trying to express:

With Yahweh as my shepherd, I will not find myself destitute. Like a good shepherd, He will find me places of safety and rest. When I am exhausted and weary, He'll find a way to refresh my spirit and renew my energy. A good shepherd will be a guide to the way I should walk. He will hear me and answer me. Even when times are tough and I experience loss and grief and death, I can be courageous, without fear, because God is a strong comfort. Not only does God prepare sustenance and celebration for me, He does it in the presence of those who hate me so we can restore broken relationships.

Although I don't like the idea of oil poured on my head, in ancient times, it was a sign of God's chosen one. And of course, a cup overflowing signifies blessings more than we could ask or imagine. Goodness and love will be the result of a relationship with the loving shepherd. We also know that it was David's priority to build the Temple of God and therefore he uses the metaphor of being in Yahweh's Temple forever.

Prayer

The good shepherd is such a appropriate symbol of Your love for us. Even we, city folk who are so far removed from flocks of sheep understand the care and the commitment that go into tending a flock. Thank You for such a vivid depiction of Your love.

_____

_____

_____

_____

_____

_____

15
hidden jewel

Facts which, at first, seem improbable, will, even on scant explanation, drop the cloak which has hidden them and stand forth in naked and simple beauty.

~ Galileo Galilei

Every promise of Scripture is a writing of God, which may be pleaded before Him with this reasonable request, 'Do as Thou hast said.' The Heavenly Father will not break His Word to His own child.

~ Charles H. Spurgeon

Lyrics

If the day and the night can be broken
So the day doesn't shine in its time
If the night and the day can be broken
I will break my promises to you

If I can't move the mountain with my mustard seed
Let me tie up my laces and climb to the peak
If my plans that seem so right shut down on me
I'll keep knocking keep climbing keep singing songs of praise

There will be a day there will be a light there will be a word
Filling up the empty spaces
There will be a time there will be a Branch there will be a way
My hidden jewel will shine like the sun

If the sand on the shores can be numbered
I will number the days I will hold you in my hand
If the stars in the sky give up their light to the night
That's when I'll give up on you

If I can't part the waters when I'm in too deep
Let me rise o'er the waves and keep my eyes on You
If I only hear silence when I call to You
I'll keep waiting keep hoping keep trusting in You

The book of Ruth was written by Samuel between the years 1011 and 931 BC. Not only does it (one), set the pattern of the Kinsman Redeemer which is the role Jesus plays in the plan of salvation (two), in a prophetic sense give the genealogy of Jesus long before his birth (three), link to Revelation chapter five, understanding that the scroll written on both sides is a deed that needs to be redeemed (four), link to Genesis 28 which Moses wrote and under the surface of the text is the genealogy as recorded in Ruth three hundred years earlier but, (six), according to Dr. Chuck Missler, the story of Ruth foreshadows the future situation of the church and its relation to the chosen people, Israel.

Naomi's husband Elimelech means "my God is King." Naomi was married to him just as Israel was in a covenant with God often referred to as a marriage. Naomi finds herself with no husband, in exile in a foreign land and living an existence of pain and sorrow. Israel broke their covenant with God and for 2,000 years were in exile in foreign lands living an existence of pain and sorrow. Ruth, a Gentile, became a part of the nation of Israel and was brought to the knowledge of God just as Gentiles (or the church) were brought to God and joined Israel as adopted children.

Boaz is the kinsman redeemer, as Jesus, who redeems the land. In that transaction, Ruth is also purchased. Ruth (church) is introduced to Boaz (Jesus) by the unnamed servant (the Holy Spirit at Pentecost). Ruth learns how to deal with the Boaz situation from Naomi (Israel). Naomi (Israel) learns of Boaz (Jesus) through Ruth (church).

Jeremiah 33

While Jeremiah was still confined in the courtyard of the guard, the word of the Lord came to him a second time: "This is what the Lord says, he who made the earth, the Lord who formed it and established it—the Lord is his name: 'Call to me and I will answer you and tell you great and unsearchable things you do not know.' For this is what the Lord, the God of Israel, says about the houses in this city and the royal palaces of Judah that have been torn down to be used against the siege ramps and the sword in the fight with the Babylonians: 'They will be filled with the dead bodies of the people I will slay in my anger and wrath. I will hide my face from this city because of all its wickedness.

"'Nevertheless, I will bring health and healing to it; I will heal my people and will let them enjoy abundant peace and security. I will bring Judah and Israel back from captivity and will rebuild them as they were before. I will cleanse them from all the sin they have committed against me and will forgive all their sins of rebellion against me. Then this city will bring me renown, joy, praise and honor before all nations on earth that hear of all the good things I do for it; and they will be in awe and will tremble at the abundant prosperity and peace I provide for it.'

"This is what the Lord says: 'You say about this place, "It is a desolate waste, without people or animals." Yet in the towns of Judah and the streets of Jerusalem that are deserted, inhabited by neither people nor animals, there will be heard once more the sounds of joy and gladness, the voices of bride and bridegroom, and the voices of those who bring thank offerings to the house of the Lord, saying, "Give thanks to the Lord Almighty, for the Lord is good; his love endures forever." For I will restore the fortunes of the land as they were before,' says the Lord.

"This is what the Lord Almighty says: 'In this place, desolate and without people or animals—in all its towns there will again be pastures for shepherds to rest their flocks. In the towns of the hill country, of the western foothills and of the Negev, in the territory of Benjamin, in the villages around Jerusalem and in the towns of Judah, flocks will again pass under the hand of the one who counts them,' says the Lord.

"'The days are coming,' declares the Lord, 'when I will fulfill the good promise I made to the people of Israel and Judah. "'In those days and at that time I will make a righteous Branch sprout from David's line; he will do what is just and right in the land. In those days Judah will be saved and Jerusalem will live in safety. This is the name by which it will be called: The Lord Our Righteous Savior.'

For this is what the Lord says: 'David will never fail to have a man to sit on the throne of Israel, nor will the Levitical priests ever fail to have a man to stand before me continually to offer burnt offerings, to burn grain offerings and to present sacrifices.'"

The word of the Lord came to Jeremiah: "This is what the Lord says: 'If you can break my covenant with the day and my covenant with the night, so that day and night no longer come at their appointed time, then my covenant with David my servant—and my covenant with the Levites who are priests ministering before me—can be broken and David will no longer have a descendant to reign on his throne. I will make the descendants of David my servant and the Levites who minister before me as countless as the stars in the sky and as measureless as the sand on the seashore.'"

The word of the Lord came to Jeremiah: "Have you not noticed that these people are saying, 'The Lord has rejected the two kingdoms he chose'? So they despise my people and no longer regard them as a nation. This is what the Lord says: 'If I have not made my covenant with day and night and established the laws of heaven and earth, then I will reject the descendants of Jacob and David my servant and will *not choose one of his sons to rule over the descendants of Abraham, Isaac and Jacob. For I will restore their fortunes and have compassion on them.'"*

Hidden Jewels

In the Bible, we encounter lists of genealogies. They aren't particularly exciting reading to most people yet, they often contain hidden treasures that reward the diligent.

In the book of Ruth, Boaz the Kinsman-Redeemer redeems the land for Naomi and he takes Ruth as his bride. If you have ever questioned why Jesus had to die for our salvation, in this little book there are brilliant gems scattered among the sand that will help you better understand God's plan of redemption.

In the festivities during the wedding celebration of Ruth and Boaz, someone declares, "and let thy house be like the house of Perez, whom Tamar bare unto Judah, of the seed which the LORD shall give thee of this young woman" (Ruth 4:12). This refers to what happened between Judah and Tamar.

In Genesis 38, Tamar had married Judah's firstborn son, Er, who died without having any children. Under Mosaic law, Judah was expected to provide Tamar her husband's brother to continue Er's line. Judah failed to provide. Tamar resorted to posing as a prostitute and tricked Judah who unknowingly got her pregnant. When confronted with the evidence, he confessed that his sin was greater than hers. Tamar gave birth to two sons, Zarah and Pharez. Both were, of course, illegitimate. The Torah instructs that an illegitimate son is to be cast out of the congregation for ten generations. The strange remark in Ruth 4:12 was, in fact, a prophecy: the tenth generation from Pharez was none other than David. And to emphasize this, the book closes with David's genealogy:

"Now these are the generations of Pharez: Pharez begat Hezron, and Hezron begat Ram, and Ram begat Amminadab, and Amminadab begat Nahshon, and Nahshon begat Salmon, and Salmon begat Boaz, and Boaz begat Obed, and Obed begat Jesse, and Jesse begat David" (Ruth 4:18-22). The inheritance of David was prophesied before the days of Samuel. But there's more.

The sordid tale of Judah and Tamar has been included in the Scriptures because this incident is significant to the Messiah's family tree. Interestingly, hidden within the text of Genesis 38, at forty-nine letter intervals, are the names of Boaz, Ruth, Obed, Jesse, and David *in chronological order*! In case you missed it: in Genesis, the first book of the Bible, we find the names of the participants of the Book of Ruth and a delineation of their descendants leading up to the royal line. How did Moses know this information centuries before the fact? The argument that these names may have been added later is weak because these names are embedded within the text and not detectable by simply reading the text.

That this aspect exists in the Biblical text is an astounding confirmation that it originated from God and not humans. There is absolutely no way that these details could have been anticipated except by Divine knowledge. In addition, the skillful manipulation beneath the surface of the text eclipses any possibility that the authors themselves were aware of these hidden words. And, having discovered these features within the text throughout the entire Bible, we can be confident that it is a "skillfully crafted integrated message-from Genesis 1 to Revelation 22."

Prayer

LORD, You have meticulously orchestrated hidden details in the Bible to prove Yourself. If we look, we will find You. That's the hardest part, to look for You. It's like a riddle. You have been giving us clues for millennia and now that we can decipher them we have to admit that they have been right before our eyes all along. When we see You, we can never unsee You.

_____

_____

_____

_____

_____

_____

16
hosea's love

This is my comfort in my affliction that your promise gives me life.

~ Psalm 119:50

No matter what storm you face, you need to know that God loves you.
He has not abandoned you.

~ Franklin Graham

Hosea: Will you be my bride
Will you come and live with me
Standing by your side
I'll be the only one you see
I will lead you all the way
I will never go away

Gomer: I will live with you
I will follow where you lead
But don't ask that you
Be the only one I need
I'm committed to your throne
But there are other thrones I kneel before
As you know

H: We can find a way
G: If you think we can I will
H: We're a family
G: All my children will be yours
But,
What do you ask? Every part of me

To throw down my mask
Let go of my fantasy
You know I can't
I won't

H: I have seen your shame
I will lift you from the pain
You who know my name
G: You know my name
H: I have come for you again
I have paid the price in full
You will come into my home
There you'll stay

G: He speaks tenderly
He has seen all I have seen
Yet he still wants me
Maybe he can make me clean
But,
What does he ask
Every part of me
To lay down my mask
Let go of my fantasy
I will return
I will return

He has torn my soul, He has torn my soul
H: I will heal your soul
G: He will heal my soul
H: You are my child
G: And you are my king
H: You are my love
G: And you are my Lord
H: You are my love
G: And you are my Lord

The story of Hosea is a story of deep emotion and suffering. It is a story of rebellion and stubbornness, commitment and heartbreak, sorrow and great love. Ask for a definition of love and sweet, pleasant words creep around the answer like tendrils. Ask for a demonstration of love and those words wilt. Love in action demands the rolling up of sleeves, getting embroiled in unpleasantness that sometimes causes injury and scars. It involves stepping into the unknown darkness, surrendering yourself and your intentions to another.

Hosea loved Gomer. His forgiveness and patience proved it. He abandoned any pride. He searched for Gomer and saved her at his own expense. Hosea had a vision that went beyond what could be seen; it was a vision of what would be. His actions were not for an immediate purpose but a future promise.

This is our story.

Hosea 3:1-3

The Lord said to me, "Go, show your love to your wife again, though she is loved by another man and is an adulteress. Love her as the Lord loves the Israelites, though they turn to other gods and love the sacred raisin cakes." So I bought her for fifteen shekels[a] of silver and about a homer and a lethek of barley. Then I told her, "You are to live with me many days; you must not be a prostitute or be intimate with any man, and I will behave the same way toward you.

Salvation's Love

In the book of Hosea, there is a wonderful story that parallels God's love for us. The life of Hosea (whose name means salvation) is the story of God's love for us. It's a story you have heard before. If not this specific story, then at least you will hear the similarities of Jesus' life whose name also means salvation. It's a story of a husband's love for his wife but it's a story embedded in an other story; the story of God's love for His people.

Imagine Israel 760 years before Jesus. Jeroboam II was on the throne of the northern Kingdom. Because of his military successes, Israel's borders spread out farther than they had been since Solomon's days. Tribute money from nations he had subdued was pouring into the treasury in the capital city of Samaria. And the people, they were enjoying a period of unprecedented prosperity.

It's no surprise that with prosperity and wealth usually come moral and spiritual degeneration, secularism and materialism. Actually, it sounds like a description of our day: swearing, lying, killing, stealing, adultery, drunkenness, perversion, deceit, oppression. What grieved God most was the nation's persistent idolatry (Hosea 4:12, 13; 13:2). The golden calves set up by Jeroboam I, about 150 years earlier, were physical signs across the land of Canaanite idolatry which included religious prostitution and human sacrifice.

Call that story "A." History. The story of a people whom God called as His own, whom He instructed and who wandered away from Him

Yahweh's relationship with Israel is best depicted with the analogy of husband and wife. Therefore, her worship of other gods was spiritual adultery. God told Israel from the beginning that He would not share her with others. The first Commandment (Ex. 20:3) is "you shall have no other gods before me." But, she had persistently ignored this command.

Enter Hosea.

The very first thing that God ever said to Hosea was: "Go, take to yourself a wife of harlotry, and have children of harlotry; for the land commits flagrant harlotry, forsaking the Lord" (Hosea 1:2). God intended to use the prophet's personal relationship with her as an object lesson of His own relationship with His unfaithful people, Israel. God directed Hosea to take Gomer, the daughter of Diblaim, as his wife.

Call that story "B." Not just a story. This is the life of a man, Hosea, whose name literally means Salvation. God breathes through the prophet's experience to speak to the hearts of His people.

At the birth of their first son, God named the baby Jezreel. It was a prophetic message to the nation because at Jezreel, King Jeroboam's great-grandfather, Jehu, had violently usurped the throne of Judah after killing all the prophets of Ba'al. While the kingdom was rid of Ba'al worship for a while, Jehu returned to worshiping idols. Destruction was on the horizon and it would happen in the valley of Jezreel (Hosea 1:4,5).

Gomer became pregnant again, this time she had a girl. God instructed Hosea to call her Loruhamah meaning unpitied or unloved. This name was again symbolic of Israel's break in loving relationship with God.

Soon after the birth of Loruhamah, Gomer conceived and bore another boy. God told Hosea to call him Lo-ammi "not my people" or "not my kin." In essence, the boy's name means, "this is not my child." The child carried the name that exposed Gomer's sinful behaviour. Hosea describes Jehovah's relationship with His unfaithful wife, Israel, as he tells his own sad story.

Eventually, Gomer left for good. She followed whom she thought she loved because they promised to lavish material things upon her (2:5). Hosea pleaded with her (2:2). He threatened to disinherit her (2:3). He tried to stop her (2:6). Gomer ignored his pleadings (2:7). Hosea repeatedly accepted her back into his home but her desires were for others and soon she wandered again. I imagine that Hosea had friends who advised him to let her go and be rid of her adulterous ways. Yet Hosea could not. He loved her and longed for her in a way that many today cannot understand. In fact, we probably deride him for being such a fool.

Eventually, Hosea heard that Gomer had been deserted by her lover and finally sold herself into slavery. Certainly, this would convince Hosea that Gomer was no good. But, he did not give up on her. God spoke to Hosea and told him to go to her even though she is an adulteress. He drew the parallel: "even as the Lord loved the sons of Israel, though they turn to other gods" (3:1).

God wanted Hosea to find Gomer and to prove his love for her. How could anyone love that deeply? The answer is in his instructions: "as the Lord loves." He began his search driven by divine love that bears all things, believes all things, hopes all things, endures all things (1 Corinthians 13).

Hosea found her: dirty, disheveled, destitute. She was a slave for sale. How could he not be repulsed? He loved "as the LORD loves." He had compassion but he also was able to see beyond the present circumstances to the future glory. He bought her for fifteen shekels of silver and thirteen bushels of barley (3:2) Then he said to her, "You shall stay with me for many days. You shall not play the harlot, nor shall you have a man; so I will also be toward you" (3:3). He actually paid for her, brought her home and eventually, restored her to her position as his wife.

We can do nothing to save ourselves. God has come to get us just as we are. Jesus paid the price, brought us back and restored us to the position we were ordained to be. He is love enough to come to you and save you just like that. You are Gomer. He is Hosea, Jesus, Salvation.

By the time Gomer heard Salvation's voice speaking to her, by the time she felt Salvation's hand loose the chains that bound her to the slave block, by the time Salvation gently lifted her from her sorrow and shame, the price had already been paid. Salvation, Hosea, had already paid the price, already made the deal, already delivered the goods; he had already come up with the agreed-upon ransom figure.

That's where we are! The price has been paid by Salvation: Yeshua, Jesus.

He lifts us out of our despair and gives us hope and according to this story, we await to be brought home and to be restored to the position of bride, wife, beloved.

Hallelujah.

I know a fount where sins are washed away
I know a place where night is turned to day
burdens are lifted
blind eyes made to see
there's a wonder working power in the blood of calvary

Prayer

Father, we read these words.

Help us to experience them.

Thank you for washing all our sins away and removing them as far as the east is from the west. In all eternity, we will never find them again.

Thank you for turning our night into day. Many of us have gone through dark times and You have brought us into Your light with healing and restoration. And, Father, some of us are in a dark time now, but we know that You are with us and there is hope and You will restore and heal.

Father we come to you with our burdens for ourselves, for our family members for our world and we ask You to lift them off of us so that we will know Your peace. Let us rest in You.

And lastly, Father, where we are blind concerning others, open our eyes and teach us to love. Where we are blind concerning ourselves, open our eyes and remove our stubborn pride and show us Your overwhelming love for us. Where we are blind concerning You, teach us Your ways and show us Your paths.

There is a wonderworking power in the blood of calvary. The power of the knowledge of Your infinite love. Let us be a changed people because we have been in your presence.

_____

_____

_____

_____

_____

17

i love Your kindness

Have you ever noticed how much of Christ's life was spent in doing kind things?

~ Henry Drummond

Blessed be the LORD for He has made marvellous His loving kindness to me in a besieged city.

~ Psalm 31:21

I love you Lord I love Your kindness
You are the rock under my feet
You are my triumph You are my laughter
Lord, You make my life complete

I will give thanks to your name
I will be humble in heart
I will wait, wait for You Lord and trust in You
I will sing praise to Your name
I will do right in Your eyes
I will sing, sing of Your love and trust in You

You're my rock and You're my fortress
You listen to my prayers
You're the reason that my soul inside me sings
Let me dwell with you forever
As I pour my heart to you
Keep me safe under the shelter of your wings
Even when I am afraid
In the lonely night me heart cries out to You
Cries out to You

You are my anchor, You are my sail
When I am weak You make me strong
You are my lighthouse, You are my beacon
You are my hope when things go wrong

I used to help my parents at Quinte Detention Centre playing the piano for a chapel service that they led. They conducted three, twenty-minute meetings that consisted of some singing, reading scripture and a devotional thought. A guard would escort approximately ten men to the chapel and lock us in as he sat outside the door listening through a grated window. After the service, the guard escorted the men back to their secure area and escorted another group of ten men to the chapel. For each new group of men, my dad preached on a different topic. This puzzled me. I asked my dad why he prepared three different talks when he really only needed one talk. He could repeat it three times. It would be new to each group of men. He pointed to the door where the guard sat.

John 4:13, 14

To the Samaritan woman at the well Jesus explained, "Everyone who drinks this water will be thirsty again, but whoever drinks the water I give them will never thirst. Indeed, the water I give them will become in them a spring of water welling up to eternal life."

Leggo My Ego

This is a transcript of an actual radio conversation of a US navel ship with Canadian authorities off the coast of Newfoundland in October, 1995.

Americans: Please divert your course 15 degrees to the south to avoid a collision.
Canadians: Recommend you divert *your* course 15 degrees to the south to avoid a collision.
Americans: This is the Captain of a US Navy ship. I say again, divert *your* course.
Canadians: No. I say again, you divert YOUR course.
Americans: This is the Aircraft Carrier USS Lincoln, the second largest ship in the United States' Atlantic Fleet. We are accompanied by three destroyers, three cruisers and numerous support vessels. I demand that you change your course 15 degrees north. That's one five degrees north, or counter measures will be undertaken to ensure the safety of this ship.
Canadians: This is a lighthouse. Your call.

The word synecdoche, pronounced si–nek–duh–kee, is a literary term. It means when the single part of some large, complex system stands for the whole. Here are some examples: asking for her hand in marriage, give us this day our daily bread, commenting on a car with, "nice wheels," when "the crown" stands for royalty.

Each of the commandments is synecdochic: each means more than itself. Each is a tiny part that stands for the large whole. So when we are commanded, for instance, not to steal, the command stretches far beyond the bare bones decree: don't steal! It means more than simply to restrain your hand from thievery. It implies the whole way of life. That little commandment, "Thou shalt not steal" encompasses a life of contentment, disciplining the appetites, becoming trustworthy and practising generosity.

Choosing not to steal, to refuse to take what does not belong to you, is barely obedience. It is certainly not life to the fullest. One can obey the letter of the law and still be a thief, hoarding, coveting, envying.

But, if you can envision the commandment in a synecdochical dimension, it becomes an invitation to abundant life. It is an invitation to be like Scrooge after his night time visitors: lavishing gifts on strangers. It is to be like Zacchaeus after Jesus came to his home: with an outburst of generosity instantly replacing a lifetime of greed.

To what things have you been responding like the captain of the US navy ship, thinking your way is the right way when God is calling you to something different?

God is going to do what He said He will do, with or without you. He is telling you today that He is the lighthouse and you may need to change our course.

Prayer

Thank you for your kindness to me in all my moments and all my experiences. I find You are my rock and my refuge and You have never let me down. I want Your help in continuing to ask for things I need in my life because I believe I don't deserve the good things that You are waiting to lavish on us.

_____

_____

_____

_____

_____

18

it wasn't the child

There are two ways to be fooled. One is to believe what isn't true; the other is to refuse to believe what is true.

~ Søren Kierkegaard

History is a set of lies agreed upon.

~ Napoleon Bonaparte

It wasn't the king
He was wrapped in his importance
Believing what he wanted to believe
It wasn't the king
Though we ridicule his name
It wasn't the king

It wasn't the swindlers
They were not deluded
They gambled all on probability
It wasn't the swindlers
Though we give them all the blame
It wasn't the same

It wasn't the loom
Left unused and empty
Those golden threads were never used
It wasn't the loom
Standing on its frame
It wasn't the loom

It wasn't the second in command
He was blind and full of fear
Obeying and doing what he was told
It wasn't the second in command
Though we chide he even came
It just wasn't him

It wasn't the child
He had no self control
A traitor to his youthful honesty
It wasn't the child
Though we contemplate his fame
It wasn't the child
It wasn't the child

I love this story. It is ridiculous. If you pay attention, you can see this story played out around you in daily life. It is a testament to the powers of peer pressure as well as the fear of social disgrace. It can be contextualized in situations where people are widely acclaimed but others question whether what they have created is of any value. Modern-day examples might be the highly-priced work of conceptual artists or the more avant-guard products of fashion designers that are clothed more in popularity than in true value. In addition, propaganda about pseudo science prohibits people to question on pain of social reprisal, public shaming or loss of status and even loss of employment, where they are silenced from speaking about what they see and pressured to keep silent.

The Emperor's New Clothes bears some similarity to another modern-day expression, 'the elephant in the room.' An essential factor with both phrases is the willingness of people to engage into an unspoken contract to willfully disbelieve what they know to be true.

Matthew 22:1-14

Jesus spoke to them again in parables, saying: "The kingdom of heaven is like a king who prepared a wedding banquet for his son. He sent his servants to those who had been invited to the banquet to tell them to come, but they refused to come. "Then he sent some more servants and said, 'Tell those who have been invited that I have prepared my dinner: My oxen and fattened cattle have been butchered, and everything is ready. Come to the wedding banquet.' "But they paid no attention and went off—one to his field, another to his business. The rest seized his servants, mistreated them and killed them. The king was enraged. He sent his army and destroyed those murderers and burned their city. "Then he said to his servants, 'The wedding banquet is ready, but those I invited did not deserve to come. So go to the street corners and invite to the banquet anyone you find.' So the servants went out into the streets and gathered all the people they could find, the bad as well as the good, and the wedding hall was filled with guests. "But when the king came in to see the guests, he noticed a man there who was not wearing wedding clothes. He asked, 'How did you get in here without wedding clothes, friend?' The man was speechless. "Then the king told the attendants, 'Tie him hand and foot, and throw him outside, into the darkness, where there will be weeping and gnashing of teeth.' "For many are invited, but few are chosen."

Diamond Ring

When I was young, I had a boyfriend. One day, he asked me to marry him. He bought me a beautiful diamond ring. Diamond rings are very expensive. It was worth a lot of money. I wore that ring on my finger and it was valuable to me, not only because it cost a lot but, because it symbolized something very special to me. Eventually, the relationship ended. We were no longer planning to be married but, he didn't want the ring back. At this point, that ring was no longer very valuable to me regardless of how much it had cost. As a matter of fact, years later, I traded it with my sister for a necklace that was worth about 1% of its total value.

The things that we place much value on are sometimes, in the end, not worth much.

Prayer

God grant me the sincerity to be honest and true, the courage to admit when others are not honest and true and the wisdom to know the difference.

_____

_____

_____

_____

_____

19

jeremiah's letter

Jeremiah was instructing the Jewish exiles to engage in intercessory prayer for their enemies and work for their well being. This message underscores that God is the God of all people—Jew and Gentile. No single racial or ethnic group; no one nation can have a monopoly on the God of all creation. God loves all people and cares for their well being.
~ Rev. Garth Wehrfritz-Hanson

Perhaps even more important than figuring out how to live amidst these less-than-perfect circumstances is the question of how one manages to find joy while being in exile.

~ Juliana Claassens

He wrote his script by the
Light of the moon
Moving from right to left
Tears in his eyes but hope in his heart
Flowing from every word he wrote

Across the miles
A boy couldn't sleep
He leaned out from his window
Searching the night looking for a hope
He saw the prophet's pen
Looked in his aching eyes
Heard a distant voice

For I know the plans I have for you says the LORD
Plans to help you not to harm you

To give you a future and a hope

He grabbed his shoes and ran
Down dusty streets
Pulled his best friend out of bed
They ran and ran to the prophet's house
Sat at his feet
The music of his words
Exploded into day

Jeremiah that old prophet
Rolled the scroll in his withered hand
And he passed it like a baton is a racer's hand
For a moment
Time stood still
To the future
To bring hope
To know God's love

For I know the plans I have for you says the LORD
Plan to help you not to harm you
To give you a future and a hope

This promise was intended for the exiles but it extends to all Jews regarding their history and to the church regarding its destiny. I think it's wonderful that God has plans to bless me and give me a future and a hope, but according to Jeremiah 29:7 that promise is tied up with me seeking the welfare of my enemy-neighbours. God wants to bless me. Part of the way that He blesses me is by calling me to be a blessing to others, even people whom I could reasonably hate.

Jeremiah 29: 1-3

This is the text of the letter that the prophet Jeremiah sent from Jerusalem to the surviving elders among the exiles and to the priests, the prophets and all the other people Nebuchadnezzar had carried into exile from Jerusalem to Babylon. He entrusted the letter to Elasah son of Shaphan and to Gemariah son of Hilkiah, whom Zedekiah king of Judah sent to King Nebuchadnezzar in Babylon.

An Encouraging Letter

We all face times when we suffer a great loss, experience grief, death, divorce, war, unemployment, financial crisis, health issues, disappointment, betrayal. These sorts of significant events cause great upheaval. They are usually overwhelming and full of grief for the way things were in the past, stress for the situation to navigate in the present and fear for the unfamiliar future.

For me, a divorce I didn't want catapulted me into single parenthood. During this time in my life, I received a letter from a family friend. He had a way of putting a new perspective on my situation. At the time, I saw my life fall in shambles around me like knocking over a bookshelf full of books. The letter that he wrote to me lifted me out of that present devastation, reminded me that it wouldn't always be that way and that in the future, things would be better.

God gave messages to Jeremiah to relay to the king, the princes, the priests and the people. However, there were other 'so-called' prophets preaching the opposite message, a message more pleasing to the ears. As a result, the king put Jeremiah in stocks and eventually in prison to be rid of him. But Jeremiah was undaunted. He knew what he was getting into when he took this job. . . when he unwillingly accepted this position. Okay, so he was given no choice in the matter (Jeremiah 1).

God told Jeremiah that King Nebuchadnezzar of Babylon was going to besiege the city of Jerusalem. It was God's will that the people of Jerusalem submit to Babylon's authority. God clearly told Jeremiah to tell everyone that if they wanted to live, they must submit to Babylon. If they did not submit, they would die from famine and devastation.

Jeremiah went to the busiest part of town, the Temple, and proclaimed God's message. The problem was that other prophets contradicted Jeremiah and predicted that Babylon would retreat, they would return what they had stolen and everyone would continue to live in peace in Jerusalem.

How did Jeremiah respond to that? He didn't. He didn't fight. He didn't defend himself. He said the way to see who is the real prophet from God is to wait and see who is telling the truth. What happened? Babylon came, destroyed Jerusalem, took many Jews away from their homes to live in exile.

For them, the way they had always lived was in upheaval; their future was uncertain. Their neatly aligned bookshelves had been toppled and the books lay in disarray at their feet. They grieved their past, were stressed about what to do in the present and were fearful of their future.

God said to Jeremiah: Write them a letter. Tell them not to worry. Tell them that the exile will last seventy years. Knowing that, they should settle down, build houses, have children, marry them off and have grandchildren and they should have more children. Work for the prosperity of whatever city you end up in. I know the plans I have for you. I am going to bless you and make you prosper in exile, not harm you. You have a future and a hope in my will.

Imagine how it would have felt, in exile, away from everything familiar, feeling lost and abandoned, to receive a letter from Jeremiah (who has been proven over and over to be the real prophet of the real God) with a message to you from God?

What more would you need in life?

Wouldn't it be great to receive a letter from God today as you face the problems, frustrations and upheavals in life? Do you wish God cared enough about you to write you a letter and comfort you about your future?

I am telling you today that He has written that letter with the words in Jeremiah, "For I know the plans I have for you, plans to prosper you not to harm you to give you a future and a hope" (Jeremiah 29:11). And God has sent not just a letter but an entire care package: the life, death and resurrection of Jesus. Jesus is the embodiment of our future hope as he repeatedly stresses that the Kingdom of God is soon coming. He outlines the end times that we are living in, gives us peace through these tumultuous times and reminds us that he is soon returning. There will be a day with no more upheavals, no more fears.

We can deal with our past griefs, have peace in our present stresses and God will calm our fears of the future because we are in God's will. His plans are to prosper us not to harm us; to give us a future and a hope.

Prayer

God of hope, how often have we found ourselves in exile, separated from Your presence! Restore us and let us find You when we seek You.

_____

_____

_____

_____

_____

_____

20

light a candle

It is better to light a candle than curse the darkness.

~ Eleanor Roosevelt

Look at how a single candle can both defy and define the darkness.

~ Anne Frank

When the night is dark
You can't find your way
Hope has lost its spark
Sky has turned to grey
When your heart is broken
Sadness in your eyes
Dreams are left unspoken
Your heart will arise

Every time the morning shines
It's a promise of a brand new day
When the light of heaven comes
You will always find your way

When your hope is shattered
No one hears your cries
Nothing seems to matter
Your heart will arise

We can't conquer greed with greed
We can't vanquish shame with shame
When your anger fills your need

Then there's no one else to blame
You don't have to be afraid
Find your answer in the right
When you need to conquer dark
The only way is with the light

When the night is dark
Light a candle
You can't find your way
Light a candle
Hope has lost its spark
Light a candle
Sky has turned to grey
Light a candle
When your heart is broken
Light a candle
Your heart will arise
Light a candle
Your heart will arise
Light s candle
Your heart will arise
Light a candle

The purpose for this song is to give hope to people who feel hopelessness. It's normal to have bad days when you think everything is wrong. But when those bad days stretch on to bad weeks and months, it's easy to get discouraged. It's easy to lose the will to continue when life has unravelled into a mess of loose strands. But for those who persevere, they find that those strands can be woven into a beautiful image, even a masterpiece.

Because I hold the belief that God brings hope and a life change, I am profoundly saddened by the death of people who take their own lives while in the depths of hopelessness. Please, if you feel that way, you need to have the key to unlock what bars you, the magic potion that transforms you. What is that key, that potion? It is hope. You need the knowledge that this is not the end of your story; you have many chapters left. Obviously, I like metaphors. Metaphors aid in understanding. This song uses the lighting of a candle to represent prayer as an act of expectation that God will rescue you as He promised.

Psalm 40:1-3

I waited patiently for the LORD; he turned to me and heard my cry. He lifted me out of the slimy pit, out of the mud and mire; he set my feet on a rock and gave me a firm place to stand. He put a new song in my mouth, a hymn of praise to our God. Many will see and fear the LORD and put their trust in him.

God The Weaver

God had a plan for Moses from birth. Moses didn't even know who he himself was let alone who God was. Events and circumstances happened. He didn't fight against them. He followed God. God wove the events of his life, all the hurts and confusion, the anger and the misconceptions together for His divine purpose and Moses turned out to lead the children of Israel across the desert to the Promised Land. He was the man whom God knew face to face (Deuteronomy 34:10). God is bigger than anyone can see or imagine.

To us, God may seem 'silent' most of the time. Those times when he 'acts' are surrounded by many years of silence. The years between Joseph and Moses are many. The years between Malachi and John the Baptist are many. The years between Jesus' first coming and his next are many. Then and now. But God is sovereign and He is working. He will "win out" even if we don't live to see it. Knowing that is peace.

God works things out. Even in the darkest, loneliest moments, God promises to give a future and a hope. And He actually fulfills that promise! Proverbs instructs, "Trust in the LORD with all your heart and lean not on your own understanding. In all your ways submit to him and he will make your paths straight" (Proverbs 3:5).

Prayer

So we turn to You when we don't know what to do. You have given us the assurance that You are present with us and You are active in our lives.

"Indeed, if you call out for insight and cry aloud for understanding, and if you look for it as for silver and search for it as for hidden treasure, then you will understand the fear of the Lord and find the knowledge of God" (Proverbs 2:3-5).

For that we come to You with gratitude; in thanks and praise for all You've done for us, for all You do and all You will do as you foretold us in the Scriptures. We ask to rely on You more and more each day and get to know You better.

_____

_____

_____

_____

_____

21
lightning

Thunder is good, thunder is impressive; but it is lightning that does the work
~ Mark Twain

Bible teaching about the Second Coming of Christ was thought of as "doomsday" preaching. But not anymore. It is the only ray of hope that shines as an ever brightening beam in a darkening world.
~ Billy Graham

I was down at the station
In the pouring rain
Without hesitation
He stepped down from the train
He was warm He was dry
He looked deep in my eyes
He sat down beside me
He motioned me near
He whispered the words
I'd been waiting to hear
There'll be wars: there'll be fears (Matthew 24)
But you won't shed a tear
Lightning will flash from the east and will shine to the west

It was silent between us
The trains had all gone
The dark in the morning was turning in to dawn
It was music It was art
He had stolen my heart
The morning commotion

Started up again
People with cases
And here comes the rain
I must go; you must stay
But you'll see me again
Lightning will flash from the east and will shine to the west

The name Zaphenath-Paneah that was given to Joseph in Egypt, is derived from the Hebrew roots: tsaphan and paneach. Tsaphan means "to hide, treasure or store up." Psalm 119 reads "Your Word have I hid in my heart," which in Hebrew is belibi tsaphanti. Paneach means "to decipher, solve, decode, interpret." Pharaoh deliberately gave Joseph a name that can be translated, "He who explains hidden things" because he explained to Pharaoh the hidden meaning of his dreams. The name Zaphenath-Paneah not only reflects Pharaoh's experience of Joseph but God's will unfolding in Joseph's life story. And if I can take it one step further, the story of Joseph contains hundreds of parallels to the life of Christ. (See appendix E).

Matthew 24:27

For as lightning that comes from the east is visible even in the west, so will be the coming of the Son of Man.

Son of God; Son of Man

Some of the ideas and doctrines we hold as Christians may not seem to make any sense. Some people choose to take it on faith and move on. Some people can't accept some of our explanations. Or maybe we don't understand things as we should. Every idea comes from somewhere. We better understand the foundations of our beliefs when we read the Bible

When you don't know the content of the Bible, it is easy for doubts to creep in. When you don't know what the Bible teaches, it is easy for others to argue with their own reasoning which can sometimes be quite convincing.

Which title has generally been used to accentuate Jesus' divinity? "Son of God." And which title has been used to accentuate his humanity? "Son of Man."

You would think.

In the book of Mark, "Son of God" referred to the King of Israel, the earthly king of David's seat while the "Son of Man" indicates that Jesus is a part of God. Son of God indicates that Jesus is the Messiah. Messiah means "anointed one." The word Christ, *christos,* is the Greek word for the Hebrew *mashiach.* In John 1:41, after meeting Jesus, Andrew declares to his brother Simon, "We have found the Messiah."

Before Jesus was born, the king who sat on the throne of Israel was called the Messiah because he was actually anointed with oil when he became king. In the book of 1 Samuel 10:1, Samuel pours a vial of oil over the head of Saul and names him king of Israel. "Then Samuel took the vial of oil and poured it upon his head, and kissed him and said, has not Yahweh anointed you to be prince over his inheritance?"

This king of Israel is appointed by God to rule Israel and to represent Israel before God. Through Samuel, God anointed Saul. Therefore, in the Hebrew Bible, the king is referred to as the anointed of Yahweh or the Meshiah of Yahweh. The following were anointed with oil when they became king:

David (1 Samuel 16:3)
Solomon (1 Kings 1:34)
Jehu (1 Kings 19:16)
Joash (2 Kings 11:12)
Jehoahaz (2 Kings 23:30)

The anointed king of Israel is adopted by God as His son: "Kings of the earth set themselves up and rulers conspire together against Yahweh and against His anointed one (His Meshiah) . . . I have installed my king on Mount Zion my holy hill. I will recount the decree of Yahweh. He said to me, "You are my son; this day I have begotten you" or enthroned you (Psalm 2:2, 6-7). The son of God is thus the reigning king of Israel. Also in Psalm 110 we find the king as the son of God.

The point in all this digging is that initially, the term 'Son of God' referred to the Davidic king but not the deity of the king. "I will be to you as a father and you will be to me as a son." The king is indeed very intimate with God but the king was never considered God like other nations considered their king a god. The kingship is promised to David's seed forever.

However, during the sixth century BC, the kingdom of God's anointed one in Jerusalem was destroyed and the Davidic line was lost. In 2 Kings 25, following a siege in 597 BC, Nebuchadnezzar appointed Zedekiah king of Judah but Zedekiah revolted against Babylon and Nebuchadnezzar invaded Judah. In 587, Nebuchadnezzar broke through Jerusalem's walls and conquered the city. Zedekiah tried to escape, was captured, watched as his sons were killed, was blinded and bound and taken to Babylon as a prisoner until his death. After the fall of Jerusalem, the Babylonian General, Nebuzaradden was sent to plunder Jerusalem and destroy Solomon's Temple. Most people were taken into captivity while some were left to remain on the land.

The people were exiled for seventy years but even when they were allowed to return, there was no longer a Davidic kingdom and no glorious king ruling in Jerusalem. The people prayed for such a king to rule over them once more and for a restoration of that earthly glory. Here, the seeds were planted for the notion of a promised redeemer, a new King David whom God would send at the end of the age.

When Mark, at the very beginning of his Gospel writes, "the beginning of the gospel of Jesus Christ, the Son of God, "the Son of God" means the human Messiah, using the old title for the King of the house of David. When on the other hand, Mark refers to Jesus in the second chapter as the Son of Man, he is pointing to the divine nature of the Christ. This seems like a paradox: the name of God being used for Jesus' human nature and the name Man being used for his divine nature. Jesus was understood as God by monotheistic Jews by telling the story of the Son of Man.

In the book of Daniel, chapter seven, there is a remarkable apocalyptic story. Apocalypse is derived from a Greek word that means revelation. The New Testament book Revelation is also called Apocalypse. Generally, the things that are revealed have to do with the end of time. That is why it is popularly used today to indicate the end of the world as we know it, as in the "zombie apocalypse."

The book of Daniel is one of the first apocalypses written. Similar to the visions of the prophet Ezekiel, it describes the heavenly visions of Daniel. In one of Daniel's visions, there are two divine figures. One is depicted as an old man, literally the Ancient of Days, sitting on a throne. There is another throne and another divine figure who looks like a human being brought in on the clouds and is invested in a ceremony by the Ancient of Days.

"In my vision at night I looked, and there before me was one like a son of man, coming with the clouds of heaven. He approached the Ancient of Days and was led into his presence. He was given authority, glory and sovereign power; all nations and peoples of every language worshiped him. His dominion is an everlasting dominion that will not pass away, and his kingdom is one that will never be destroyed" (Daniel 7:13).

The text describes a second divine figure to whom will be given eternal dominion over the entire world, a restored world. The king's rule will be in accordance with the will of the Ancient of Days. Jesus taught his disciples to pray: "your kingdom come, your will be done on earth as it is in heaven" (Matthew 6:10). This redeemer figure is divine. He is in human form. He is portrayed as younger than the Ancient of Days. He will be enthroned on high. He is given power, dominion and sovereignty on earth. All of this Daniel saw almost 200 years before the birth of Jesus.

This idea of an expected return of a Davidic king and a divine ruler in human form gave rise to a divine-human Messiah. He was named "Son of Man" alluding to his origins in the book of Daniel. When we read, Son of Man in the gospels, it alludes to the vision in the book of Daniel.

Jesus refers to himself as the Son of Man. When Jesus walked in Galilee proclaiming himself as the Son of Man, no one ever asked, "What is the Son of Man?" Whether or not they believed it, they knew exactly to what Jesus was referring.

In ordinary Semitic usage, son of man simply means "human being." One would think that the people in Aramaic would just hear him calling himself human, a person. But the context in Mark goes beyond that. For instance, when Jesus said, "the Son of Man has authority on earth to forgive sins" (Mark 2:10), he was not saying that any person has the ability to forgive sins. Or when he said that the "the Son of Man is Lord even of the Sabbath" (Mark 2:28), he was not saying that any person is lord of the Sabbath.

It makes sense historically and literally that the "Son of Man" was a recognized title to the writer of Mark and to the people of Jesus's day. Where did it come from? The answer is the book of Daniel. If Daniel is the prophecy then the gospels are the fulfillment. The Son of Man is an entirely heavenly figure who becomes a human being.

The Son of Man was so named even before the universe came into being. The Son of Man will be worshipped on earth by all who dwell on the earth. He is the Anointed One, the Messiah, Mashiah in Hebrew and Christos in Greek. The Son of Man occupies the throne of glory seated at the right hand of the Ancient of Days. All of the functions assigned to the divine figure called "One like the son of man" in Daniel 7 are given to the one who is called the Christ.

I am not telling you anything new. The Christian church has been proclaiming this for over 2,000 years and the Jews, well the Jews, who have had these truths embedded in their writings for over 3,000 years are telling the same story we hear every week when we come to church: Jesus is the Messiah and he is coming again. Yes, you read correctly. There are some exciting things happening in Israel today. We cannot remain ignorant of them. Our future and our faith depend on it.

There is a growing movement introducing Jews in Israel and around the world to their Messiah. Chapter fifty-three of Isaiah has been largely ignored by rabbis in the prescribed weekly readings. When reading the words of Isaiah 53, Jews understand that Yeshua, Jesus, fulfilled those prophecies in Isaiah and identify him as Messiah. This in itself is fulfillment of prophecy. I am quoting from a Jewish, website: "While Ben-Gurion (the founder and first prime minister of Israel) and Netanyahu's longing for Israel to fulfill its mandate to be a light to the world may seem lofty to some; it is actuality God's plan."

It has been fulfilled in Yeshua HaMashiach (Jesus the Messiah), the Jewish Messiah who is the Light of World (Isaiah 42:5-7; John 9:5). Israel has fulfilled this mandate and in the time to come, will fulfill this calling in even greater measure when it nationally recognizes Yeshua.

"And I will pour out on the house of David and the inhabitants of Jerusalem a spirit of grace and supplication. They will look on Me, the one they have pierced, and they will mourn for Him as one mourns for an only child, and grieve bitterly for Him as one grieves for a firstborn son" (Zechariah 12:10).

The geographical restoration of Israel foreshadows greater miracles: the spiritual restoration of Israel and the physical return of Yeshua to Israel as King Messiah. We are living in fascinating times as we see prophecy fulfilled.

God wrote the Bible. We know this because it tells history backwards. It tells the end from the beginning. God told us He was going to do this so that when the events happen, we will remember that He told us and believe that He is God (John 16:4).

He has told us the end from the beginning. We are living in those times when the events are coming to pass. Jesus admonished that no one knows the day or the hour but we can figure perhaps that the seventh millennium of our history will belong to Jesus the Messiah. Jesus said, "Look, I am coming soon! My reward is with me, and I will give to each person according to what they have done" (Revelation 22:12).

Prayer

Even so, come Lord Jesus. Come.

_____

_____

_____

_____

_____

_____

22

l'ombra dell'passato

It is by no means an irrational fancy that, in a future existence, we shall look upon what we think our present existence, as a dream.

~ Edgar Allan Poe

My yesterdays walk with me. They keep step, they are gray faces that peer over my shoulder.

~ William Golding

Lyrics

Le pietre messe insieme sono case in una storia	The stones together are houses in a story
La gente tutti insieme move come la mia ombra	People move in tandem like my shadow
La ragazza che camina strappando i versi in mano	The girl who walks is tearing verses in her hand
Il vecchio gira in giro aiuta come può	The old man walks around helping where he can

Dai un occhiata	Look!
Quando ti giri è tutto	When you turn around, it's gone!
Senti le campane	Listen to the bells
Suonano soltanto qui nell'ombra della notte	They only sound in the shadow of the night

Le sento da lontano in un tempo sbagliato	I hear them from a distance in the wrong time
Ma loro non mi possono sentire	But they can't hear me
Allungo la mane nella nebbia per toccarli	I extend my hand in the fog to touch them
Non c'è la faccio	I can't reach them

Ti appoggi sul muro tutto sudato	You lean on the wall all sweaty
La luce poderosa non ti dice dove sei	The powdery light won't tell you where you are

| Il muro, la strada, non fanno più rumore | The wall, the street, make no noise |
| Aspettano attese la musica che viene | They wait in anticipation for the music that is to come |

| Ho perso il mio cappello nell'acqua corrente | I lost my hat in the current |
| Prima il fume poi il mare poi l'oceano immenso | First the river, then the sea, then the immense ocean |

When Harry Potter receives a letter from Hogwarts, there is a glint of hope in his eyes; hope that is dashed each time another letter arrives and Dursley rips it from Harry's hands or tears it to pieces. As readers (or viewers), we are horrified to see how Dursley continues to rise massively between the boy and his destiny. Emotions rise as letter after letter streams into the Dursley home. Owls relentlessly deliver the same letter. When the owls are gathered all around the house, we understand that they will not stop until Harry gets the message.

Despite Dursley's attempts to keep Harry in despair, he cannot succeed. Hundreds of letters flood the room and we feel a surge of elation and maybe even let out a little squeal looking around self-consciously. When Hagrid bursts the door down to remove Harry from his squalor, we are out of our chair with our fists in the air shouting, "Yes! Yes!."

Because this is the way it should be. This is the way it will be!

James 4:14

Why, you do not even know what will happen tomorrow. What is your life? You are a mist that appears for a little while and then vanishes.

Deep Needs Need Deep Resources

My husband and I took our children to our city zoo. There are places to picnic, fun animals to see and a play park. Best of all, it's free! The play park has swings, a waterpark, a climbing apparatus and a long, tube slide.

I watched as children waited in line for their turn down the slide. It looked like fun so I waited in line for my turn and plopped myself in the tube. It was a long way down. Weeee. Once at the bottom, you have to come back by climbing a series of many steps. I felt energetic so I took those stairs two at a time. I reached the top and was surprised that I was not panting. I went down again and again, undaunted by those stairs.

After the third time running up those stairs two at a time, I noticed that I was indeed panting and my heart rate was climbing. I prefer not to sweat and pant unless absolutely necessary. I began to wonder how long a rest period I would need until I could run up the stairs without panting again.

In order to answer that question, I had to understand what happens between the first and third times I run up those stairs. Could I rest long enough between climbs to never have to pant and sweat again?

Here is what happens: the ATP (adenesontriphosphate) in the muscle gets broken down into ADP (free phosphate). The breaking of the bond releases energy that turns into movement so muscle cells can contract. Following a quick burst of exercise, the body needs to restore the ATP. The body can metabolize food energy, glucose, and fatty acids, It starts to metabolize right away.

When you send a message to the muscles to move, a signal that is proportional to the intensity of that signal gets sent to the heart and lungs. The first time, you get a little response. The second time and the third time, you are accessing deeper energy stores. You are depleting any energy in the cells plus depleting glucose. But the fourth time, there is a generalized body response and it needs to recruit stored energy.

If you are like me and you don't like sweating and panting, it may be your personality to maintain balance. I like things right at the fulcrum: not too extreme one way or the other. Not too much joy; not too much pain. Not too much stillness and not too much excitement.

A routine that maintains equilibrium can provide a false sense of security and an equally false assumption that you have strength of character. Things may seem alright while you are tapping the mild energy source. You may be getting by when your needs are manageable. But, when situations become stressed, when relationships become intense, when pressure mounts from responsibilities, the mild energy source is not enough to meet the high energy needs. In stressful times, we need to be able to access a deeper energy source; one that won't be depleted.

We can appear strong when not taxed by any intense need. Throw some problems in (the car breaks down on your way to work) and some deep needs (finding a place to live, losing your mate, a sick child) then we need a deeper source of energy. Proverbs 3:5-8 says it plainly: "Trust in the Lord with all your heart and lean not on your own understanding; in all your ways submit to him, and he will make your paths straight. Do not be wise in your own eyes; fear the Lord and shun evil. This will bring health to your body and nourishment to your bones."

Prayer

Lord, strengthen me to trust You with all my heart because I know You, what You have promised and what You will do. Once I know that, I will lean on You and not my own understanding. Trusting You will heal my restlessness and my anxiety. Trusting and knowing You will refresh my tired bones and give me life anew.

    Thank You

_____

_____

_____

_____

_____

_____

23

l'ultima preghiera

My prayer for you is that you come to understand and have the courage
to answer Jesus' call to you with the simple word, 'yes.'

~ Mother Teresa

I call you to prayer on this issue. Sometimes we struggle but, have we
really been faithful in prayer on this issue? We have a faithful God.

~ Mark Hall·

When does this road end that we're travelling
When does the bluebird finish his song
Will you always be a memory
Will you stay away so long

You were still in the midst of the dance
You were silent when everyone sang
You were alone
When we were together
You remained when all was gone

And I pray
Even though I know I know my way
Still I say
A prayer for you
A prayer for you

Lungo la strada della vita   Long is the road of life
Ci siamo incontrati dopo un po'   We met after a while

Magari non siamo stati insieme molto	We may not have been together long
Uno sguardo un sorriso no so	A look, a smile
E io prego	And I pray
Anche quando so che conosco la via	Even when I know I know my way
Dico sempre	I always say
Una preghiera, una preghiera per te	A prayer for you
Devi sapere	You must know
Nel mio cuore	In my heart
Ogni giorno penso a te	Every day I think of you
Ogni giorno della vita	Every day of my life
La mia ultima preghiera sarà per te	My last prayer will be for you
L'ultima preghiera sarà per te	

There are membranes around the esophagus that hold it in place so that the esophagus does not move. That makes sense. You don't want your esophagus moving around. However, the membranes around other organs such as liver, kidneys and intestines, for example, are slippery because in their function, these organs necessarily move. When patients undergoing surgery need their intestines set outside the body then replaced, doctors inevitably cannot return the intestines to the exact original position. Miraculously, the intestines eventually re-situate themselves in the correct configuration to resume their function.

What this fascinating fact means to me is that God has established functions in the body that we may never need and yet, when the situation arises, our bodies have already been programmed to respond. That, to me, is an expression of love by our Creator.

James 5:16

Pray for each other so that you may be healed. The prayer of a righteous person is powerful and effective.

E-mail

I am thankful for the concept of e-mail. Whoever invented electronic mail must understand prayer. Electronic mail is the perfect analogy for prayer for these reasons: you type your message from anywhere to anywhere, you can be in your home or at work or on your phone half way across the world and when you press send, it goes, well, somewhere to instantly show up in another's inbox. Like prayer, there is no specific place you have to be. You can be anywhere and you can send it anywhere. When we pray, we don't really know where our prayers "go."

It's possible to communicate with someone we know nothing about or to the most intimate friend you have. Similarly, with prayer, we can talk to God whether it is our first time or our millionth time.

You send the email and you wait. Sometimes the answer comes back right away and sometimes it takes a long time. The best part is that, with each reply, you get to know the person better. Each reply reveals something about the sender. I can choose how often, what to communicate, how deep to get, or just to stay in touch. But God is the ultimate in courtesy. He always responds . . . eventually. And it is through prayer and watching Him work in my life through that vehicle of communication that I have been able to have a relationship with God.

Email is uncertain, unexplainable and a little mysterious but it is an experience many people are comfortable with today. Prayer is the same. Many use it effectively without understanding how it is possible.

Prayer

Thank you for the awesome privilege of prayer. I don't understand how I can talk to You and You hear me and honour my petitions. I don't understand how You orchestrate our lives. Thank you for Your mercy and Your love.

_____

_____

_____

_____

_____

_____

24

meaning of my silence

Speech is of time, silence is of eternity.

~ Thomas Carlyle

I wish you to write a book on the power of the words and the processes
by which the human feelings form affinities with them.

~ Samuel Taylor Coleridge

I've never let the words
Carry out the colours in my heart
Maybe I've been afraid
Of the silence that snuggles
Between our laughter and our
Voice

Now I've quieted my soul
LORD I know You're here
There's something in the silence
That makes me
A part of You

But when You called
I didn't answer
I heard You say
I love you
But I sat smiling, still and silent
Am I afraid to look inside
And find I love You too?

Before I called You answered
I heard You say
I love you
Jesus hear me when I don't dry
Please take my hand and look inside
And find I love You too
And find I love You too

Prophets who have had an encounter with God describe His "voice" like the sound of many waters. What does water sound like? I imagine the rush of Niagara Falls or a mighty river tumbling over rocks or the splatter of rain on the ground.

Could it be the drops tapping on the leaves as they fall through the lattice trees? Or the warm summer rain drumming on the mud? Or the lines of wind-driven rain like pointed arrows screaming through the air? Or the deafening torrents pounding like dark drumbeats? Or the tinkle of the last tired drops tintinnabulation in the remnant pools and puddles?

I was outside during the last rainstorm and I noticed that the rain had pitch and harmony, articulation and intensity, like a rock band. That's it! Maybe the prophets were trying to express that God's voice is like the sound of many rock bands!

Isaiah 66: 4

When I called, you didn't answer.

Swear Words

Do you know any swear words? This is a rhetorical question. Don't shout them out while you are reading. If I were to ask you which swear words are popular today, would you say them? Probably not because we have been taught not to say rude and hurtful things. Yes, most swear words are rude and hurtful.

Why do people use swear words? Because swear words have *power*. Isn't that interesting? They have power in two different ways. *One*: swear words significantly affect feelings and ideas. If you did sit ups and push ups everyday what would happen? You'd get strong. You'd be "ripped;" you'd have six pack abs. If you eat junk food every day and do not exercise your body, you would have a different configuration of abs. Using swear words affects you. Swear words change you. They can turn you into something else. *Two:* swear words affect others. The purpose of swear words is to shock or hurt other people and to make everyone wince and feel bad. It's like using a knife or a sword or a stick against others.

How do swear words get this power? They are socially constructed. They are given power by the general complicity of society. My sister and I once tried to start the use of a new expletive. It did not catch on. These were the days before internet. Who knows? Perhaps today, we would see a different outcome.

As a child, only my parents spoke to me in Italian. I didn't have contact with Italian friends or family. I didn't read Italian books. I didn't know any Italian swear words. When I began to read in Italian and to meet Italian friends, I saw and heard words that I didn't understand in context. My mother was horrified when I asked about these strange words because she understood them as swear words. They didn't have any meaning to me. They didn't hold any power for me because I was not a part of the culture that uses them in that way.

As a woman, I observe a harshness among males, young an old, in the use of sexual language. During my career, I have taught in public schools. I have heard the use of raunchy words increase and their vehemence intensify. I wonder what the effects of such language use has on young girls in their development. A sexual reference might be used when wanting to indicate negative connotations or derogatory put-downs or as an expression of violence, anger and hatred. As a man, one might feel empowered by such language. But, as a woman, especially a young woman, hearing the constant negative use of sexual language, how must that impact her concept of sexuality? Negatively, I would guess.

For example, commonly, parts of the male anatomy are used in name calling to indicate someone is stupid, mean or inconsiderate. These parts become tainted with negativity, derision and repulsion. When it comes time for a girl to engage with the male body, she may be more likely to view the experience tainted with negativity, derision and repulsion. In my experience, few people speak glowingly or respectfully of such things.

As well, men flippantly make jokes about female anatomy. It has become popularly acceptable to call the worst and the lowest by female parts. It seems as though we have worn out the harshest words and have replaced them with words that still have shock value. Girls who grow up hearing degrading references to their body parts before they have a chance to develop a healthy attitude toward all that the sexual experience comprises, are bound to foster distaste concerning themselves, men and the sexual experience.

I believe we need to be aware of how language psychologically affects us. Instead of speaking heedlessly, we should be mindful to use language deliberately for a desired effect. I understand that someone who chooses to be respectful is fighting against the cultural current because swearing is celebrated in some venues: movies, television, in the street, at the mall, in work places and at school. We might start to think that it has become irrelevant and no one cares anymore if people swear. But people care. There are still some things that are not acceptable to say in public. People get fired for using hurtful swear words in a professional setting and in work environments. It is not acceptable to use swear words. Still, swear words are used readily.

Swearing represents a deliberate choice to be rude. It is a message that says, 'I want to hurt you and treat you with disrespect.' It also indicates a limited vocabulary and the inability to use the language creatively. An excellent literary example is the dialogue in Cyrano de Bergerac by Edmond Rostand. When the Viscount tries to insult Cyrano by stating that his nose is very big, Cyrano derides him and gives his own creative suggestions how he could have used language more eloquently to make his insult more effective (See Appendix A).

If words have power and if our culture gives swear words the power to hurt, there must be an opposite to swear words. Which words have the power to do good and to heal? Can you think of some?

I understand
I care about you
I'm sorry
Please
It's alright
I forgive you
I will be your friend
You can join us
I love you

The Bible is called God's Word. Do you ever wonder why? Words have the power to change people's lives. They provide the power to know God's plan and to understand what is going on in our world.

Jesus is also called the Word of God in John 1:1. Do you ever wonder why? Jesus has the power to come into our lives and teach us about God and change our lives for the good. We know that words have the power to hurt or to heal. Let's decide to use good *words*, read God's *Word* and get to know *the Word*.

Prayer

Your words are full of creative power. A word from You and creation changes. Help us to learn the power of our own words and to use them for help and healing.

_____

_____

_____

_____

_____

_____

25

no one like You

In order to find God, you have only to look around.

~ Paulo Coelho

I gave in, and admitted that God was God.

~ C. S. Lewis

I have searched the foreign hills to find the rising sun
Many faces calling me turning me around
Stones give birth to men of war marching single file
A hatless man on a rainy street shakes his fist against the sky

I've seen the balls of fire raining down from the martyrs' tomb
Silence shrouds the city walls children stare
Each face is marked with darkness no one can see
A faceless god in an empty sea, is that all You are to me

My heart of stone
Replaced with a heart of flesh
You can change my speech
To a pure speech

And when I come full circle to the place where I began
Brotherhood conspiracy the mountains and the sand
Anyone can tell you it's not what you see that stands
For all my searching I have found
There's no one like You

A.W. Tozer wrote, "Men may flee from the sunlight to dark and musty caves of the earth but they cannot put out the sun. So men in any dispensation despise the grace of God, but they cannot extinguish it." There are some things that are relative to one's perspective and some things that are not relative to one's perspective. Some things just are.

Micah 7:18

Who is a God like you, who pardons sin and forgives the transgression of the remnant of his inheritance? You do not stay angry forever but delight to show mercy

Olofactory Glands

We have recently acquired a dog and I walk with her on the country roads around my house. She is some kind of a hound so she ambles down the road with her nose to the ground. And she doesn't walk in a straight line. She veers off to the left into the woods and to the right in the middle of the road. She stops and sniffs. Initially, I thought she was faking. What could there possibly be to smell on a paved road?

We went for a walk early one morning after the first light snowfall, before any car tires marred the surface. I saw tracks made by deer that had crossed the road over night. I saw imprints of a small rabbit dance and I saw what I think were wolf or coyote tracks venturing out of the woods and leading back in. She hadn't been faking at all! I hadn't been able to see what she knew for a fact. It wasn't until the snow revealed what had been there all along that I saw what she was detecting with her olfactory glands.

Ever wonder if God is real? If Christianity is just another religion? Do you ever wonder if God acts in our world? I've talked to people who can't see any evidence of God and who believe He does not exist. One of the things that proves the veracity of God and His word is prophecy. He told us the end from the beginning. That allows us to see the way He has worked in the past and is still working in our time. We know that God did some amazing things in the Bible like signs and wonders to bring the Israelites out of Egypt, fighting battles for them in the past and keeping them safe in Israel today as they face missiles, bombs and terrors from all sides.

We remember what God did in Egypt with the 10 plagues each defeating an Egyptian god (See Appendix B), culminating with the death of the firstborn. The angel of death passed over those who killed the lamb, ate it with bitter herbs and unleavened bread and spread its blood over the door posts. Those protected by the blood of the lamb escaped death.

Why do I think this is proof? Passover is still celebrated *every year* as Moses commanded them in Exodus over 3500 years ago.

"This is a day you are to commemorate; for the generations to come you shall celebrate it as a festival to the Lord—a lasting ordinance. For seven days you are to eat bread made without yeast. On the first day remove the yeast from your houses, for whoever eats anything with yeast in it from the first day through the seventh must be cut off from Israel. On the first day hold a sacred assembly, and another one on the seventh day. Do no work at all on these days, except to prepare food for everyone to eat; that is all you may do. Celebrate the Festival of Unleavened Bread, because it was on this very day that I brought your divisions out of Egypt. Celebrate this day as a lasting ordinance for the generations to come" (Exodus 12:13-17).

God guided them through the wilderness with a pillar of cloud by day and a pillar of fire by night. He gave them manna to eat in the desert and water from the rock in a dry land. For forty years they did not falter or grow weary. Their clothes didn't wear out. The sandals on their feet didn't wear out. Their feet did not get swollen and sore from walking in the desert heat.

God explained to Moses that He did these things not only to bless them and to fulfill His promises to Abraham hundreds of years earlier but in order that all the nations of the world would see and know that God is the Creator. He told them to teach their children. Further study into the Passover and the Feast of Unleavened Bread shows without a doubt that this event, which is still celebrated today around the world, is point by point, date for date, fulfilled in the life, death and resurrection of Jesus Christ. (See Appendix C).

Prayer

Lord, there is no one like You who forgives, loves, knows the end from the beginning and tells in advance what will happen so that when it happens we will remember You told us and finally believe You. Thanks. You are amazing. There is none like You.

_____

_____

_____

_____

_____

26

on and on

God is not in such a hurry as we are, and it is not his way to give more light on the future than we need for action in the present, or to guide us more than one step at a time. When in doubt, do nothing, but continue to wait on God. When action is needed, light will come."

~ J.I. Packer

Rivers know this: there is no hurry. We shall get there some day."

~ A.A. Milne, Winnie-the-Pooh

Lyrics

Haven't you heard
Don't you know
The One who made heaven and earth
Who can compare
There's no one like Him
Trust in His power in your life

Why do you think
He can't carry your load
He's Creator and Eternal Father
He gives strength to the weary
People just like you
Trust in His promises
He promised

They that wait upon the LORD
Shall have strength anew

They shall fly with eagles' wings
They shall run on and on

Isn't it time
You rest in His care
Lay your burden on His love
There is power and hope
Forgiveness and rest
Trust in His promises
He promised

They that wait upon the LORD
Shall have strength anew
They shall fly with eagles' wings
They shall run on and on

I've been on this kick lately, claiming God's promises. He said that His words will not return to Him empty, which to me means His words are not like our words. They are alive and they create. They are motion. They affect things and change things. He promised. He will keep His word. The promise in Isaiah 40 is one of those promises that I have to claim often. I will wait on the LORD and I wait for His strength to do what He has asked me to do.

Isaiah 40:31

They who wait on the LORD will renew their strength. They will soar on wings like eagles, they will run and not grow weary, they will walk and not faint.

Revel in Healing

Jesus and his crew were in Capernaum and Jesus taught in the synagogue on the Sabbath. He was different from the scribes and Pharisees. People recognized that something was different. He spoke like he knew what he was talking about. He had authority. You can tell when someone speaks with authority.

In the crowd was a man with an "unclean spirit" that gave him grief. Jesus cast it out of him and the demon recognized Jesus. He told the demon to be quiet and to not give him away. Is that not curious to you? At once, Jesus' fame spread.

They went to Simon's house after 'church.' His mother-in-law had a fever and Jesus removed it. She used her renewed health to serve them. That night many sick, diseased and demon-possessed came to Jesus, swarmed him and he healed them all. But he wanted the demons to be quiet because the demons recognized him. (!)

I wonder what it was about Jesus that made him such a great healer. Of course, I have the luxury of wondering that because I am not sick or demon-possessed. If I were sick, I would go to him, too, in the hope of being healed and I wouldn't question my healing. I wouldn't wonder. I would revel in my healing and used my renewed health to serve others.

This was the beginning of his fame. People depleted him with their needs. They took all they could from him. He gave until there was no more to give and in giving his all, we are satisfied, we can be satisfied and we will be satisfied.

The truth is that God loves us beyond our comprehension and He has everything that we need.

Prayer

What more can I say but, "thank You?" It always comes down to this. You amaze me and I can't thank You enough.

_____

_____

_____

_____

_____

_____

27

once more

> Love is the only force capable of transforming an enemy into a friend.
> ~ Martin Luther King Jr.

> I see the world being slowly transformed into a wilderness. I feel the
> suffering of millions. And yet, when I look up at the sky, I somehow
> feel that everything will change for the better, that this cruelty too shall
> end, that peace and tranquility will return once more.
> ~ Anne Frank

When the time is right
And the time is now
When the LORD speaks
And the past is past
Who is left who has seen the mighty works of God
Who is left who has seen the mighty works of God

With the work that is here
And I AM is with us
By His word
Promised long ago
While my Spirit remains among you do not fear
While my Spirit remains among you do not fear

Once more
In a little while
I will shake the earth
I will shake the heavens
Once more

In a little while
I will shake the seas and
I will shake the mountains

He shall come
The Desire of Nations
I will fill this Temple
I will fill this Temple with glory
He shall come
The Desire of Nations
I will fill this Temple
I will fill this Temple with glory

The silver is Mine
And the gold is Mine
And the next shall be greater than the first
All the silver is mine
And the gold is mine
And the next shall be greater than the first

And in this place
In this place
I will give peace
I will give peace

It is a bold statement at the end of the Noah's Ark story to claim that God promised never to flood the earth again (Genesis 9:11). What would be the result if the world were to flood any time after the Noah's time? The entire Bible would be considered a fraud. Only God could make such a promise. The claim that God will not give up on Israel is a bold declaration indeed; a claim only God can make.

Haggai 2: 6-9

This is what the Lord Almighty says: 'In a little while I will once more shake the heavens and the earth, the sea and the dry land. I will shake all nations, and what is desired by all nations will come, and I will fill this house with glory,' says the Lord Almighty. 'The silver is mine and the gold is mine,' declares the Lord Almighty. 'The glory of this present house will be greater than the glory of the former house,' says the Lord Almighty. 'And in this place I will grant peace,' declares the Lord Almighty.

Gifts

Birthday parties are great, aren't they? Who doesn't like birthday parties? Everything about birthday parties is wonderful. Balloons, cake, all your friends in one place, gifts. Gifts symbolize the relationship between you and your friends. I don't mean a better friend gives you a more expensive gift. The very giving of a gift represents friendship and caring. What are good gifts? What kind of gifts have you received or given? What have been memorable gifts?

The great thing about a gift is that you don't have to give it back. When I attended university, I went to the bank and some very nice people seemed to want me to go to school as much as I wanted to go to school. They gave me money but when I was done school, I had to pay it back . . . and then some . . . for years. That money was not a gift.

A gift does not have to be expensive to be important. The true value of a gift is not measured in money. When it brings happiness or if it fills a need in your life, it has great personal value.

God has given us many gifts but His greatest gift is the ransom sacrifice of His son, Jesus Christ (Matthew 20:28). This is the most valuable gift you will ever receive because it can bring unlimited happiness and fill your deepest, most important needs. It is the ultimate expression of God's love for us. This ransom is God's way of delivering us from sin and death (Ephesians 1:7).

In order to understand the value of this gift, we need to understand what Adam and Eve lost for us when they sinned. When God created Adam, he had perfect human life. Perfect body, perfect mind, no sickness aging or death, a special relationship with God as with a father, fulfilling purpose, work to do: all the things we long for.

Adam was made in God's image (Genesis 1:27). People have qualities like love, wisdom power, justice. We were not created like a machine to perform mindlessly; we have the ability to make decisions. When Adam disobeyed God, he was condemned to death. He paid a high price. His sin cost his perfect human life affecting subsequent generations (Romans 5:12). Through one man's sin, death entered the world. The Bible says he sold himself into sin and death (Romans 7:14).

Ransom is a price paid to release someone (prisoner) or the price that covers the cost of something (damages). Since perfect human life was lost, no imperfect life could buy it back. What was needed was a ransom equal in value to what was lost (Psalm 49:7,8). Another perfect human life was required (1 Timothy 2:5,6).

God did not send just anyone to do the duty. He sent His only begotten son, the one most precious to Him. (1 John 4:9,10). Willingly, Jesus left his heavenly home (Philippians 2:7). Jesus was perfect human life and never sinned. He was called the last Adam (1 Corinthians 15: 45). He gives hope, life and peace. (Romans 5:19 and 1 Corinthians 15:21, 22).

Jesus paid the ransom by his suffering and death (Hebrews 10:10) once and for all. On the third day, God raised him back to life (Hebrews 9:24). God accepted the value of the sacrifice Jesus made as the ransom needed from our slavery to sin and death (Romans 3:23,24).

What can this mean? We still suffer disease, age and death. Despite our sinful human condition, we can still enjoy the blessings of the ransom: forgiveness of sin and a clean conscience before God. Forgiveness allows us to worship despite our imperfections. We can approach the throne of God boldly in prayer (Hebrews 4:14-16) and in the hope of everlasting life (Romans 6:23). The wages of sin is death but the gift of God is everlasting life bought through Jesus Christ the Lord (Romans 6:23).

All future blessings including perfect health, mind, body and a perfect relationship with each other and with God are made possible by the death and resurrection of Jesus. Appreciate it and get to know the One who facilitated it (John 17:3 and 1John 5:3).

The next will be greater than the first. The next what? The next Temple, the next coming of Christ, the next creation, the next life.

Prayer

I love how You expose what will happen through the writings of a selection of people. Your word came through men and women from widely different backgrounds, experiences and ages. Each story corroborates Your story creating a unity that can only be of supernatural origins. You have gone to great lengths to have the evidence ready when we arrogantly accuse You. Thank You for Your patience.

_____

_____

_____

_____

_____

_____

28

only in a song

Words make you think. Music makes you feel. A song makes you feel a thought.

~ E.Y. Harburg

All deep things are song. It seems somehow the very central essence of us, song: as if all the rest were but wrap pages and hulls!

~ Thomas Carlyle

Only in a song only in a dream
Only in a story can we know what this all means
Only in a song only in a dream
Only close your eyes to see where you have never been

Don't stack all your gold into nice neat piles
Don't put all your money in a drawer
Use it spend it give it all away
Make somebody smile that's what gold's for
Everybody talked about
Everybody laughed about
The guy who said things in a peculiar way
He made you raise a brow
Made you tilt your head
Made you look at things in a different way

Even if you find the narrow door
Will you be able to get through
And when you do don't be surprised to see
The narrow road is what it opens to

Good things happen when you're sad
There's a reward when things go bad
There's no reward for good so let it pass
Illusions for our eyes disappearing in our hands
Light the way but they elude our grasp

There is no end to the treasures found by reading the Bible. It is God's active and living Word. It changes the thoughts, hearts and lives of those who encounter it. The stories have meaning on the surface. There is depth of meaning between the lines. There is meaning embedded beneath the surface of the literal text for those with lenses to see it. There is also meaning as the stories are overlaid on events in time. There is seemingly no end to the layers of discovery.

Matthew 6:33

But seek first his kingdom and his righteousness, and all these things will be given to you as well.

Blessings

Christmas shopping one year, I did an extraordinary job at keeping expenses low. I bought a craft for the neighbours, a book for my mom, sweatshirt for my dad, dollar store items for my kids and their bus driver. I thought I did great. Each time I bought a gift, I felt proud of myself for not spending much. I knew I was doing well. And then, I added it all up! It surprised me how much I had actually spent.

That same surprise awaits us when we count our blessings. The difference is our perception: how we feel things are going and how they are truly going. Taking an account creates a clearer picture of reality. There is no doubt that God has blessed us. We can take an account by listing some now: food, clothes, family, freedom, friends, talents, security, ability to read, music, special relationships, opportunities and so on. In Genesis 12:1-3, God called Abraham and promised to bless him and make his name great. He promised to give Abraham blessings: sheep and cows (wealth), influence, power, servants, knowledge and family numbered as the stars.

What is most striking is what comes after the promise to bless Abraham. What comes after, defines the purpose of all those blessings. God promised to make Abraham a blessing. What is he going to do with all those sheep and cows and servants, knowledge and family? He is going to become a blessing to others.

Josephus writes that Abraham excelled in mathematics, science and astronomy. He travelled and shared his knowledge with the wisemen of his day. When he was in Egypt, he explained things to them and they listened to him. He had the ability to teach and persuade.

As we know, the blessing of his son, Isaac, and subsequent descendants were eventually to bless all nations through the culmination of the plan of salvation through Jesus Christ. Abraham is the father of three faiths and has influenced nations, generations and cultures throughout the ages. God certainly fulfilled His promise to Abraham. I believe, this message is for us today as well.

God has blessed us and He will make us a blessing to others. Think of the list of blessings we counted at the beginning. How can each one of them become a blessing for others? We can share some of what we have with others. Your experience shared might encourage someone who is struggling with the same thing. Your friendship and compassion might help someone who is going through a difficult time. God wants to bless us and make us a blessing.

Prayer

I do see Your gifts to me as having the purpose of being used to bless others. Thank you for all You do to support me and maintain me. Let all that You do for me be a blessing to others.

_____

_____

_____

_____

_____

_____

29
prince of peace

Why did Christ come into the world? To liberate people from sickness, troubles and from death. In its essence, Christmas is a holiday of hope.
~ Vladimir Putin

How can mankind achieve a lasting peace? True peace of heart, mind and soul can only come through Jesus Christ.
~ Mitsuo Fuchida

Angels in the sky abound tonight
Echoing the trumpet sound
Whispering Messiah's name
He is born in Bethlehem

Showers in the grass won't wait tonight
God has sent a saviour here
Lifted up our hearts and hands
He has brought the victory

Come and worship Christ the King
From a lowly manger
To the ruler of everything

Quietly we waited long this time
Hoping in a heavenly light
Waiting for the holy babe
He has come to us this night

Come and worship
Christ the King
From a lowly manger
To the ruler of everything
Prince of Peace
Forevermore is He!

This song was written for Christmas but it is worth meditation and reflection anytime especially in the climate of our current world conditions.

Micah 5:5

And he will be our peace when the Assyrians invade our land and march through our fortresses. We will raise against them seven shepherds, even eight commanders.

Peace

Peace is generally defined as the existence of healthy relationship and the absence of conflict. The word "peace" comes from the Latin "pax" which means freedom from civil disorder. The English word came to be used in various personal greetings from 1300AD as a translation of the Hebrew "shalom." Peace can also mean an individual's sense of self: peace of mind. As well, it intimates a quiet reflecting and a calm, serene approach to life that avoids quarrelling and seeks tranquility.

Is there peace in the world? Not now. Look at headlines from recent news stories depicting struggles, violence and malice on international, national, local and personal levels. We are nowhere near peace in the world according to the above definitions.

But notice that even in our definitions of peace, we ignore God. We leave Him out of most things in our culture. We no longer fight against Him, argue with Him or rebel against Him. We just quietly ignore Him. We don't want to mention Him in our schools, on the radio or tv unless we are swearing. Being correct these days means we don't talk about God. In reality, there can be no peace without God. Just as God is the definition of love so God is also the definition of peace. God is love. God is peace.

During the Christmas season, we gather to celebrate advent peace, what are we celebrating?

Advent means 'coming' and we must be anticipating the coming of Peace. Isaiah 9:27 says, " . . . the increase of his government and of peace there will be no end."

The one whom God will send, the Messiah, will bring peace with him, will be peace and peace will be the theme of his government. Is there now or has there ever been any government great or small that has brought peace to the people and to the nations? No. So we are still waiting for this Messiah to come.

Many think Jesus was the Messiah and he already came and that's why we celebrate Christmas. Although Jesus fulfilled many Messianic prophecies there are other prophecies he did not fulfill. "The wolf and the lamb shall feed together; the lion shall eat straw like the ox" (Isaiah 65:25). "They shall not hurt or destroy in all my holy mountain" (Isaiah 65:25). "The earth will be filled with the knowledge of the glory of the LORD as the waters cover the sea" (Habukkuk 2:14). "The lamb in the midst of the throne will be their shepherd and he will guide them to springs of living water and God will wipe away every tear from their eyes" (Revelation 7:17). "Behold the dwelling of God is with men. He will dwell with them and they shall be His people and God Himself will be with them, He will wipe away every ear from their eyes and death shall be no more neither shall there be mourning nor crying nor pain anymore for the former things have passed away" (Revelation 21:3,4). "Your king comes to you triumphant and victorious is he, humble and riding on a donkey . . . and he shall command peace to the nations; his dominion shall be from sea to sea and to the ends of the earth" (Zechariah 9:10).

Why are we celebrating Jesus if he hasn't done this?

Traditionally, these advent preparations were in anticipation of the coming of Messiah. In our day, we spend four weeks before Christmas preparing for the first advent but it doesn't make sense because he already came. Why prepare for something that has already happened? On the contrary, we must prepare for the future coming of Messiah in our time.

When Jesus was on earth in the flesh, he touched many people's lives and brought them peace. He healed people, (the centurion's son, the woman with the issue of blood, the blind, the lame, the lepers). He strengthened the faith of those who were plagued with doubt (Zacchaeus, Peter, Thomas, Mary and Martha) and he caused peace and spoke about peace (calmed the storm and the demoniac among the caves, "my peace I leave with you" John 14:27). That is all in the past, a murky and difficult to understand past. Most of us are not lame and blind and possessed.

If you want to know what real peace is, read Micah 5:5 again. "And he will be our peace when the Assyrians invade our land and march through our fortresses. We will raise against them seven shepherds, even eight commanders. They shall rule the land of Assyria with the sword and the land of Nimrod with the drawn sword, and they shall deliver us from the Assyrian when he comes into our land and treads within our borders."

When we go home at the end of the day and relax with a good book or a hot drink, that is not peace. When we go about our lives in the absence of turmoil, that is not peace. We don't need peace when there is no trouble. When all is calm, we coast without agitation. That is not peace; that is a void of turbulence. Peace is not the absence of something. Peace is something.

But, when we are agitated, under pressure, under attack, when friends turn, when our families let us down, when government and laws are against us, when the enemy gets the best of us, when the Assyrians are within our borders and trample on our land, literally or figuratively, then we need something. Then peace is something: the assurance of God's sovereignty.

Peace is the knowledge that God is present with us and active; active in our personal lives and active globally. Peace is a very present truth in our lives. God with us, Emmanuel. But peace is also knowing that in a certain time in history, when what was foretold happens, we don't need to be afraid because God will raise up men and princes to be victorious. And mostly, kingdom shall rise against kingdom and nation shall raise against nation and the judgment of the LORD shall come when Messiah comes to reign. We can lift up our heads without fear because we will have the peace of God in us.

That is peace. Emmanuel. God with us. Remember Messiah's lowly birth in a manger and look forward to Messiah's reign of eternal peace which will come soon.

Next Christmas, as we put together the nativity scenes and sing carols to a baby born over 2000 years ago, let's remember that Christ is our peace because he is Emmanuel, God with us, and he is coming to this planet to establish his rightful government. His kingdom shall know no end.

Prayer

We do not live in a peaceful world whether we live in war time or not. Even when there is an absence of war, there is no inner peace. The challenge is to remain still and know that You are God. My prayer is to rest in You to know Your peace amongst the turmoil of this life.

_____

_____

_____

_____

_____

30
secrets

Blessed are the cracked for they shall let in the light.

~ Groucho Marx

Jesus promised his disciples three things: that they would be completely fearless, absurdly happy, and in constant trouble.

~ William Barclay

He was called the man of sorrows
But he brought joy inside my heart
He promised us tomorrow
And he gave me a new gave me a new start

He told the secrets everyone should know
About his heavenly Father how He loves us so
There will be a new creation and
Jesus will reign

You know the kingdom of heaven
Is like a mustard seed
It is the smallest, the smallest seed
Full grown it is a tree
And the birds
Of the air
Make their nest inside its branches

You know the kingdom of heaven
Is like a fishing net
You throw it into the water

Watch all the fish you get
But you pull it up and
Sort through it
Separate the good and bad

You know the kingdom of heaven
Is like a business man
Who found a pearl of great value
Searching through the land
In order
To buy it
He sold everything he had

He was called the man of sorrows
But He brought joy inside my heart
He promised us tomorrow
And He gave me a new gave me a new start

He told the secrets everyone should know
About His heavenly Father how He loves us so
There will be a new creation and
Jesus will reign

How do you communicate that you love someone? You can tell them, hug them, treat them well. You can do those things because you are the same. A hug, a word, a smile translate to love because we are human and those things mean the same thing to the receiver as they do to the sender.

How do you communicate to a cat or a dog that you love them? You treat them right, feed them, pet them, open the door when they knock. (We have a cat that knocks at the door when he wants in). We are not exactly the same but we are similar in many ways because we are mammals. In this case, touch and affection translate to love for both orders.

How would you communicate to an ant that you love them, if indeed you loved an ant? Scratch your head about now. We are not the same in most ways. As a matter of fact, we don't have very much in common with an ant. My son, still quite young, answered this question by saying, "I wouldn't step on them. But, how would they ever know? They continue their little lives never knowing how close they were to death; never knowing I saved them."

Matthew 13:11

He replied, "Because the knowledge of the secrets of the kingdom of heaven has been given to you, but not to them."

Secret Messages

Through the prophet Isaiah, God says, "My ways are not your ways and my thoughts are not your thoughts. As the heavens are higher than the earth, so are my ways higher than your ways and my thoughts higher than your thoughts" (Isaiah 55:8,9). God is very different from us, even more different from us than we are different from the ant. If God wanted to communicate to us that He loves us, how would He do it?

I believe that God has left us secret messages everywhere and most of the time we are not aware of them. We walk right by them and we don't even know it. But every once in a while, we stumble across one of the messages and we have to pause and be amazed. God really loves us and He's trying to communicate that to us. I will let you in on three secret messages.

Have you ever accidentally cut yourself, maybe a paper cut or a slip with scissors or in the kitchen while chopping vegetables? What do you do for a cut? You put a bandaid on it. The bandaid represents the first secret message. When you get a cut, your skin opens and blood comes out. Do you bleed to death every time you cut yourself? No. You stop bleeding. Why?

Every time you cut yourself, eight or nine different things have to happen before the blood clots and you stop bleeding. Reading all the steps involved in the process of blood clotting takes longer than it takes to stop bleeding. (See Appendix D).

Scientists look into their microscopes and see this process and they are amazed. Somebody designed us this way. He must really love us to take care of us so well. And to think, this happens even when we aren't aware of it. And there are many more marvellous, miraculous ways God has left secret messages in our body that He loves us.

Let's get out of our body and look at where we live: our earth. Do you know that there are forces on the earth that are in such delicate balance that if anything changed even slightly we'd all be dead?

If the earth were slightly closer to the sun, we'd burn up. It would be too hot to live here. If the earth were slightly farther away from the sun, we'd be frozen. It would be too cold to live here. If gravity were any less, we'd float away. If it were any more, we'd be too heavy to move.

People look out from their telescopes and they learn this and are amazed. This is planned and designed and whoever set this up must really love us. The telescope represents the second secret message.

My very dear friend said to me that the balance of the fundamental forces is enough to make him think twice about being an atheist. God even speaks to atheists! All this happens even when we are not aware of it. And there are many more marvellous, miraculous ways God has left secret messages on our planet and in our universe to show that He loves us.

Remember we couldn't figure out how to communicate with an ant to let them know we love them? Well, I thought of a way. What if we could become an ant, learn to speak their language and understand their little habits? That would work.

The third way God has left us a secret message of His love is by sending his son Jesus to live among us, speak our language and understand our little habits. For God so loved the world that He gave His only begotten son that whosoever believes in Him shall not perish but have everlasting life" (John 3:16). For this, we don't need a microscope and we don't need a telescope but we do need to open our eyes and learn about Jesus. We do that by reading or listening to the Bible. And when we do, we are amazed. Somebody designed this plan so precisely that He must really love us. And many more marvellous, miraculous ways God has left secret messages in the Bible that He loves us.

These messages exist even if we walk through our lives blindly and never become aware of them. The messages all say the same thing: God loves us!

Prayer

Open our eyes Lord. We want to see Jesus. These "secrets" have been there all along. It's amazing to be able to see them with new eyes!

_____

_____

_____

_____

_____

_____

31

send the rain away

See what variety of methods the great God takes to awaken sinners to repentance by convincing them of sin, and showing them their misery and danger by reason of it.

~ Matthew Henry

God looked for justice ([~mishpat] in Hebrew) but received bloodshed, or oppression, ([~mispah] in Hebrew). God looked for righteousness ([~tsedakah] in Hebrew) but received a cry ([~seakah] in Hebrew). This play upon the contrasting meanings of similar words is called paronomasia . . . much of the force of such contrasts is lost in translation from one language to another.

~ James Burton Coffman

Send the rain away
Let the children play
Let the fire fall
On another day
Undeniably call
Send the rain away

He's a stranger in our land
Seeds he planted with his hand
On a stoney ground made a way
Spilled the water every day

He saw it all from his tower
But he never saw a flower

He shook his head and he frowned
Shut the gates and left town
His land was deserted
What should have grown was perverted

When I recorded this song, I explained to Barry, the producer, what the metaphor was: God was so disheartened with His people that he was going to stop the rain as a result of their disobedience. When I heard the final version of the song, Barry had added the sound of rain at the end of the song. Rain doesn't belong. The whole purpose of the song is the emotion of God rejecting His stubborn rebellious people. But, the rain represents forgiveness. I like that better than the stand I wanted to take with this song. Barry saw the heart of God better than I did with my heart of stone. God says, "I will not be angry forever . . ." (Isaiah 57:16).

Isaiah 5:1-6

I *will sing for the one I love*
   a song about his vineyard:
My loved one had a vineyard
   on a fertile hillside.
He dug it up and cleared it of stones
   and planted it with the choicest vines.
He built a watchtower in it
   and cut out a winepress as well.
Then he looked for a crop of good grapes,
   but it yielded only bad fruit.
"Now you dwellers in Jerusalem and people of Judah,
   judge between me and my vineyard.
What more could have been done for my vineyard
   than I have done for it?
When I looked for good grapes,
   why did it yield only bad?
Now I will tell you
   what I am going to do to my vineyard:
I will take away its hedge,
   and it will be destroyed;

I will break down its wall,
*   and it will be trampled.*
I will make it a wasteland,
*   neither pruned nor cultivated,*
*   and briers and thorns will grow there.*
I will command the clouds
*   not to rain on it."*

Reflection

The story in Isaiah 5 begins without identifying the vineyard and the owner. Once the story is told, the reader is asked to judge. At this point, Isaiah reveals that he is speaking for Yahweh (who else commands the clouds vv5,6)? The reader now understands that God planted the vineyard; the vineyard represents Israel and Judah.

In the Hebrew language, the poetry uses paronomasia which are similar paired words to contrast what God wanted and what He received. As noted in the quotation used at the beginning of this chapter, God looked for justice (mishpat) but received bloodshed, or oppression (mispah). God looked for righteousness (sedakah) but received a cry (seakah).

What a disappointment to entrust your greatest treasure to those who do not recognize its value. Not only do they not recognize its value but they despise, defile and destroy it.

Prayer

Thank you for Your forgiveness, Father. I don't want to take Your forgiveness for granted. It cost You the ultimate price and I want to appreciate its life-changing power in my life. What I mean is, because I recognize that You have forgiven me, I want to turn to You and that naturally means loving and forgiving others. It costs me to forgive, too. So thank you for the rain!

_____

_____

_____

_____

_____

_____

32
silence

A baby is something you carry inside you for nine months, in your arms for three years and in your heart till the day you die

~ Mary Mason

If one feels the need of something grand, something infinite, something that makes one feel aware of God, one need not go far to find it. I think that I see something deeper, more infinite, more eternal than the ocean in the expression of the eyes of a little baby when it wakes in the morning and coos or laughs because it sees the sun shining on its cradle

~ Vincent van Gogh

Jumaani

A toy in a stream or an ocean liner
Both designed for launching
Balloons released by a tiny hand
Escape into the sky
Coloured caterpillars wrapped up tightly
Emerge and mount the current
I release my fear-tight grip
O Lord my God
By faith into Your plan

O Lord, Your power cannot be measured
You guard the feet of the faithful
So they will not be moved
Take this child of mine
O Lord, my God

And fulfill in him Your promises
Mold his will into Your plan divine
As we give him back to you

Skaai

My lovely baby sleeping in my arms
You will rest in the shadow
Of the ever-present Lord
And when you feel the longing
For comfort in this world
You will know I'm beside you
Forever I will guide you
By His word

Forever I'll see you as the child I know now
Though you turn into a woman I'll
Have to understand
That the years go round and round they go
But somewhere in-between we grow
Wherever life finds you
Forever I will guide you
By His word

Father in heaven we kneel before Your throne
You have given us this precious gift
For our very own
And we ask that all we do and say
Will help her carry on her way
And wherever life finds us
Forever we will guide her by Your word.

Canaan

When we doubt, forgive
Where we lack, please give us Your grace
Every step we take

May Your Spirit dwell within us
May our past declare all Your righteousness
And our future rest in Your promises
May we speak tenderly
And see Your face in the small things
May we show gentleness
And watch Your power unfold
May we be selfless and kind
In our hearts may You find
Silence
And stillness
And love

Each of these songs was written for the dedication of my children in chronological order and I had the privilege of singing each song at their respective dedication ceremonies in the Salvation Army. At one point, my children thought that all kids have their own dedication song. Maybe all kids should.

1 Samuel 2 (RSV)

Hannah also prayed and said,
"My heart exults in the Lord;
*   my strength is exalted in the Lord.*
My mouth derides my enemies,
*   because I rejoice in thy salvation.*
"There is none holy like the Lord,
*   there is none besides thee;*
*   there is no rock like our God.*
Talk no more so very proudly,
*   let not arrogance come from your mouth;*
for the Lord is a God of knowledge,
*   and by him actions are weighed.*
The bows of the mighty are broken,
*   but the feeble gird on strength.*
Those who were full have hired themselves out for bread,

but those who were hungry have ceased to hunger.
The barren has borne seven,
    but she who has many children is forlorn.
The Lord kills and brings to life;
    he brings down to Sheol and raises up.
The Lord makes poor and makes rich;
    he brings low, he also exalts.
He raises up the poor from the dust;
    he lifts the needy from the ash heap,
to make them sit with princes
    and inherit a seat of honour.
For the pillars of the earth are the Lord's,
    and on them he has set the world.
"He will guard the feet of his faithful ones;
    but the wicked shall be cut off in darkness;
    for not by might shall a man prevail.
The adversaries of the Lord shall be broken to pieces;
    against them he will thunder in heaven.
The Lord will judge the ends of the earth;
    he will give strength to his king,
    and exalt the power of his anointed.

Hannah

The story of Hannah begins by explaining that she was married to Elkanah, a man who had another wife, Penninah. Unfortunately, Hannah desperately wanted a child. Penninah had children. Elkanah was an upright, godly man. He went to the Tabernacle at Shiloh every year to worship the LORD Almighty. He gave portions of the sacrificed meat to Penninah and all her sons and daughters. But, to Hannah, he gave a double portion because he loved her best and he felt sorry that she did not have any children. The situation gets worse. Hannah was ashamed that she did she not have children. Penninah harassed her constantly because she had children and Hannah did not. This went on year after year until Hannah was so upset at Shiloh that she could not eat. When people get so upset they cannot eat, it is usually a sign of depression. Hannah was suffering from depression as a result of years of constant bullying.

Elkanah tried to comfort her. He encouraged her to eat. In order to get her to stop weeping he said, "Am I not more important to you than ten sons?" There is no answer recorded in the

Bible. We can imagine what Hannah's emotional state would have been. She wasn't thinking about all the other blessings in her life

Once the eating and drinking at Shiloh was over, Hannah went to the altar and poured out her heart to God. Her lips were moving but her voice could not be heard. She was in intense prayer. Eli, the priest, saw her and immediately assumed the worst. She had to defend herself and tell Eli that she was not drunk. She was expressing her grief and imploring God for an answer. When Eli understood, he blessed her and said, "Go in peace and may the God of Israel grant you what you have asked of Him." That blessing turned her around. She went away, ate something and her face was no longer downcast.

Eli's words of encouragement and blessing gave Hannah a new outlook on her problem. At that moment, she knew that she was going to have a baby and that God had a plan for him. In time, Hannah conceived and had a son named Samuel saying, "Because I asked the LORD for him." Three years later, when the boy had been weaned, Hannah and Elkanah brought Samuel to Eli and gave him to the service of the LORD.

Hannah thought she was asking for a child for herself, to end her barrenness, to end the ridicule and to end the inferiority she felt before her husband. Instead, she bore a child in God's will. That child was Samuel. God used Samuel to lead Israel as a judge and a prophet. He replaced Eli as Priest when Eli died. He was the one who anointed Saul as the first king of Israel. Samuel also anointed King David as God's chosen to be the one from whose line the Messiah would come.

From the story of Hannah, a mother of faith, we can learn that God reveals His plan for us when we turn our hearts to God in prayer.

Prayer

At the time, my prayer was for Your guidance and folding these kids in Your will. Now, I am at the point in my life (and theirs) that I have seen the fulfillment of Your promises. I am full of thanks and adoration.

_____

_____

_____

_____

_____

33

struggle to believe

There is more light in Christ's words than in any other human words. This is not enough, it seems, to be a Christian: in addition, one must believe.

~ Andre Gide

It is not as a child that I believe and confess Jesus Christ. My hosanna is born of a furnace of doubt.

~ Fyodor Dostoyevski

To believe the sun is shining when the clouds are cold and grey
To decide to keep on moving even though you've lost your way
To hold on to see with only love's eyes when we are deceived
We are called to make these choices in the struggle to believe

At times it may seem hopeless to believe at all
Every step leads to a stumble and each stumble to a fall
Pride turns us into stone so we cannot concede
Oh we need to make these choices in the struggle to believe

We need to hear these words
From a child's voice
Echoing like thunder
Music through the noise

To continue with our eyes closed and cold hearts made of stone
To perpetuate the erroneous ridiculous preposterous belief
That I am someone and there is something
When I have nothing and there is nothing to fear

To decide to see things beautiful when everything goes wrong
To believe in a melodious invigorating song
Discerning what the eyes can see and only the heart knows
When we finally make these choices in the struggle to believe

The story is about Naaman the leper and his struggle to believe. Funny how, most of my life was spent in a state of doubt and disbelief. I know that God honoured that I trudged along waiting to better understand, hoping that it would be clear to me someday. Each story and each book of the Bible is a piece of the puzzle that tells the same story. It is only in perseverance, much like putting a jigsaw puzzle together, that the image begins to emerge from the fog of our doubt and disbelief. Persist; clarity will come.

2 Kings 5: 11-14

But Naaman went away angry and said, "I thought that he would surely come out to me and stand and call on the name of the Lord his God, wave his hand over the spot and cure me of my leprosy. Are not Abana and Pharpar, the rivers of Damascus, better than all the waters of Israel? Couldn't I wash in them and be cleansed?" So he turned and went off in a rage.

Naaman's servants went to him and said, "My father, if the prophet had told you to do some great thing, would you not have done it? How much more, then, when he tells you, 'Wash and be cleansed'!" So he went down and dipped himself in the Jordan seven times, as the man of God had told him, and his flesh was restored and became clean like that of a young boy."

Why Did You Doubt?

We believe a lot of things that we don't understand. You can probably think of many. Here are a few examples: Jesus walked through a wall. Jesus is both God and man. The sun stood still for Joshua. Even though we believe, our faith is small and our faith is weak at the best of times. But God is faithful. Paul writes in 1Corinthians 1:9, "God is faithful." Yay!!

When Peter recognized Jesus walking on the water, Peter asked Jesus to call him to join him on the water. And Jesus said okay and called him out. When Peter sank, he called on Jesus again this time, to save him. Once he was safe, Jesus asked him, "Why did you doubt?"

I'm sure Peter spent a long time asking himself that question. I came up with some reasons why we doubt:

- experts say this
- experts say that
- experts don't agree
- I have always thought this
- people who believe that are weird
- it's different from what others think
- there are contradictions
- too many things interfere with the transmission of the story
- the waves engulfed me
- family has always done it this way
- peer pressure
- it asks too much of me
- it's too difficult
- I didn't have enough evidence to convince me otherwise

Regardless of why Peter doubted, the story has a happy ending. Peter knew enough to call out, "Jesus save me" and he did.

God will not leave us in turmoil. He will not ignore our cry. He will not turn away and leave us in a storm of confusion and doubt. The storm will subside and we will be saved. The answers, the directions and the assurances of His presence are there; quietly there.

Perhaps the world seems random to you. Perhaps that randomness seems to contradict a God who would be a God of order not randomness. Randomness is meaninglessness. Meaninglessness is hopelessness which causes anguish. Let's re-adjust the focus and take another look at randomness.

Try rolling two dice. At first, it seems that the results are meaningless - - just chance. But if you roll the dice enough times and record each result, a pattern of ratios starts to emerge. "If you roll dice enough times you definitely will see "streaks" of numbers, like a run of high or low numbers or something." If you roll a single die, each roll is equally likely. That means if you roll a lot, over time, you'll roll each side about as often as the others. The more you roll, the more you'll tend towards the average, collectively." Even what we believe to be an uncontrolled act behaves according to mathematical order.

Have you ever seen termites in the daylight? They seem to haphazardly meander here and there in every direction changing their course this way and that way. It is dizzying. But if you watch for hours or days, an order emerges from the apparent chaos. Soon great towers have been collaboratively constructed all without a foreman, a union or coffee breaks.

God is here. Eternity is among us (Psalm 121). We don't need to go out searching for it. To illustrate this concept, imagine the number line. We seek eternity at the outer edges of the number line. We can count negative integers into eternity past and at the other end, we can increase integers into eternity future.

However, if we look *between* the numbers in our present, we will find infinity. Between the numbers 2 and 3 there is an infinite amount of possibilities. You can cut it in half and in half again and in half again and never reach the end of numbers within the distance between 2 and 3.

Similarly, the nature of light baffles us. Light behaves as particles and at the same time behaves as waves. How is that possible? Is it waves or particles? It is both. That's hard to grasp. Nonetheless it is so.

Jesus' question to Peter was not intended to be answered the way I answered it. Why do we doubt? It was meant, I think, as if to say, "You didn't need to doubt." But, for doubters, he holds out his arm, his victorious right arm (Isaiah 41) and offers proof, security, assurance, safety, love, fulfillment, understanding, peace, joy, grace, forgiveness (Isaiah 51:12-16) in abundance.

Prayer

Even believing is a struggle but, thank You for Your perseverance and tenacity.

_____

_____

_____

_____

_____

_____

34
wall of fire

Just as your earthly house is a place of refuge, so God's house is a place of peace.

~ Max Lucado

Prayer is a strong wall and fortress of the church.

~ Martin Luther

I will be a wall of fire around you
I will be the glory within you

I lifted up my eyes and saw
An angel in the sky
He was headed to Jerusalem
I had to ask him why
He said I'm measuring Jerusalem
That city broad and bold
But before he finished answering
Both of us were told,

I will be a wall of fire around you
I will be the glory within you

I heard the voice continue like
The thunder in the rain
Send me to the scattered seed
To comfort them again
All of those who listen are the
Apple of My eye

You will know the LORD has sent you
You will know the reason why

We will call on His name
And He will answer
He will call us His own
And we will call the LORD our sovereign God

Behold the day is rising when
The LORD your God will come
There will be no cold or frost
Little children won't be lost
The living waters flowing from
Jerusalem undone
He'll be king over all the earth
No more walls and nor more curse

I will be a wall of fire around you
I will be the glory within you

One thing is unmistakable, the Bible, gives a clear and confident sense that God has a plan for this planet and He has revealed it. Over and over He promises. He unveils what He will do. In fact, I have lost count of all the "I will . . ." statements He makes throughout the Bible. Who else could claim such promises with confidence? He was alive when these claims were made and He will be alive when they are fulfilled. We, on the other hand, have no such guarantees. We have to trust in His overarching existence and rest in the knowledge He so graciously has given to prove Himself again and again. He owes us nothing yet He lets us in on this wonderful secret. "I will . . ."

Zechariah 2:1-5

Then I looked up, and there before me was a man with a measuring line in his hand. I asked, "Where are you going?" He answered me, "To measure Jerusalem, to find out how wide and how long it is." While the angel who was speaking to me was leaving, another angel came to meet him and said to him: "Run, tell that young man, 'Jerusalem will be a city without walls because of the great number of people and animals in it. And I myself will be a wall of fire around it,' declares the Lord, 'and I will be its glory within.'

Enemy Care

At our church we have something called Community Care Ministries. I guess that means we care about our community. Who is in our community that we should care about? Mothers, fathers, children, the homeless, the poor, those affected by disasters like floods and fire, the sad, the lost, those with problems, those who are sick and hungry.

Is there anyone in the list above that we have forgotten? How about our "enemies"? Jesus said to take care of the poor and the sick and those in prison. He also said to love your enemies and pray for those who are mean to us. Because we are Christians, we don't declare ourselves as anyone's enemy but there may be people who think they are our enemy. Jesus said we are to take care of our enemies. Rise above the conditions that define us as enemies and take care of them.

Interestingly, in the prayer that Jesus taught us to pray, he juxtaposes two ideas. "Give us this day our daily bread" which reminds us that God takes care of our needs making bread a symbol of sustenance and of caring. Then right after that, he asks God to forgive us just the same way that we forgive others (Matthew 6:9-13).

Sometimes, it's easier to forgive a friend than to forgive someone who we think is our enemy. But Jesus said we should. Proverbs 25:21 says, "If your enemy is hungry, give him bread to eat. If he is thirsty give him water to drink." Being enemies poised against each other ideologically or politically is not enough in God's eyes to withhold kindness and generosity. Being an enemy does not preclude showing God's love to one another. When God tells us to love one another (1 John 4:7,8), there are no limits. The rest of the Lord's Prayer continues, "Your will be done on earth as it is in heaven." That's what Zechariah is talking about in these verses.

Prayer

I look forward to the day when these words, too, come to pass and we watch before our eyes the fulfillment of Your plan. You are awesome!!!

_____

_____

_____

_____

_____

35

who will listen

If we were permitted to reason consistently in religious matters, it is clear that we all ought to become Jews because Jesus Christ our Saviour was born a Jew, lived a Jew, died a Jew and he said expressly that he was fulfilling the Jewish religion.

~ Voltaire

Listening to God is far more important than giving Him your ideas.

~ Frank Laubach

O Listen
Now God wants to tell you
He came from the Father
And he bore our sorrows
Although we despised him
To God he was beautiful
We rejected his great love
We denied the power above
And looked the other way
And looked the other way

Still God's plan continued
He became an offering for sin
He pled with God
God forgave for his sake
Although we despise him
To God he is beautiful
Jesus rose he lives again
We will rise and live again

Who will listen now
Who will listen now

Throughout the Bible, Hebrew names not only conveyed literal meaning (Obadiah means servant) and prophetic meaning (like Hosea's three children), they also reflected a person's character and identity. Therefore, there is significance when someone's name is changed. For example, God changed Abram to Abraham, Sarai to Sarah, Jacob to Israel and Jesus changed Simon's name to Peter. For this reason, it is good to familiarize ourselves with Hebrew roots and the meaning of Hebrew names even if only to add a new dimension to our understanding of the context.

The name Israel, *Yashar- El*, has as its root, *yashar* meaning straight, honest, honourable. Added to the suffix *El* it translates to a righteous or God-fearing person. Contrast that to the name it replaced, Jacob or Yakov, the root *akov* meaning crooked, and we better understand his character development. Israel is the crooked one who God makes straight (Isaiah 40:4).

Isaiah 53: 1-6

Who has believed our message
　　and to whom has the arm of the Lord been revealed?
He grew up before him like a tender shoot,
　　and like a root out of dry ground.
He had no beauty or majesty to attract us to him,
　　nothing in his appearance that we should desire him.
He was despised and rejected by mankind,
　　a man of suffering, and familiar with pain.
Like one from whom people hide their faces
　　he was despised, and we held him in low esteem.
Surely he took up our pain
　　and bore our suffering,
yet we considered him punished by God,
　　stricken by him, and afflicted.
But he was pierced for our transgressions,
　　he was crushed for our iniquities;
the punishment that brought us peace was on him,
　　and by his wounds we are healed.

We all, like sheep, have gone astray,
  each of us has turned to our own way;
and the Lord has laid on him
  the iniquity of us all.

Any Way You Slice It

Interestingly, Isaiah 53 is the chapter that is changing the minds of Jews all over the world. Previously, rabbis ignored this passage as they couldn't explain the suffering Messiah but, as prophesied, the eyes of God's people are being opened and more are recognizing Yeshua, Jesus as the Messiah.

In the story of Joseph in Genesis, there are hundreds of parallels to the life and events of Jesus. It's a fascinating study and I encourage you to investigate. (See Appendix E). One particular event is significant to my immediate discussion: when Judah repented, Joseph could not restrain himself any longer. He had to reveal himself. It will be the same when Israel nationally repents for rejecting Yeshua. Jesus himself will return to this planet and gather his people and all the predictions in the Bible will have come to fruition.

Prophecy is not just predicting events that will happen. Prophecy is alive. Everything that God does is prophetic. Is it code? Enigmas? Riddles? Puzzles? All of the above. And the answer to all of these is Jesus. Every discovery points to the gospel story encapsulated in John 3:16. "For God so loved the world that He gave his only begotten son that whoever believes will not perish but have everlasting life." This is the theme buried within the mechanics of the Bible.

For example, here is a list of Adam's descendants and the meaning of their Hebrew names: Adam means man. Seth means appointed. Enosh means mortal. Kenan: sorrow. Mahalel means the blessed God. Jared: shall come down. Enoch means teaching. Methuselah means his death shall bring. Lamech means the despairing. Noah means rest or comfort. How intriguing that the names of the first ten generations create a sentence. Not only do they create a sentence, the content of the sentence leaves us open-mouthed:

"Man is appointed mortal sorrow but the blessed God shall come down teaching. His death shall bring the despairing comfort or rest."

The essence of the gospel story is established in Genesis in a manner that no one can dispute. God has hidden these things throughout the Bible to convince this arrogant, unbelieving, atheistic generation we live among that He indeed is the author of the Bible. Even in isolation, this gem is proof that God (Yahweh) is the author of the Bible and that God's plan from the beginning was to send Jesus to restore creation.

God has planted hidden gems in other places to convince us that He is who He said He is. The number seven is mentioned repeatedly throughout the Bible. Whether or not we understand the symbolism fully, we can agree that the number seven is special, significant and symbolic. The number seven continues to emerge outside the Bible in our physical and social world.

White light is made up of seven colours. In music, there are seven notes in the diatonic scale. The human body is completely renewed every seven years. Sabbath is the day of rest every seven days. God declared our years to be three score and ten (10x7). The period of human gestation is 280 days or 40 x7. Gestation for other animals follow a similar pattern: mouse and hen - 21 days (7x3), rat, hare and duck - 28 days (7x4), cat - 56 days (7x8), dog 63 days (7x9), lion - 98 days (7x14) and sheep - 147 days (7x21).

I used to quietly scoff at the idea that God dictated the Bible word for word. Because I am used to reading the Bible in English, I believed that the general principles were from God but that they reached us with variations based on cultural interpretations influenced by individual values. I was humbled, however, when I discovered that the original Hebrew and Greek provide a different perspective. Firstly, the original Hebrew miraculously, has not changed over the centuries.

God chose the Jews for many reasons: to bless the world with the Messiah, to be a template of heavenly things through their festivals and the Temple, and to preserve His word for all time. If you think that this is just a metaphor or a social reflection of our own idea of God, or a personification of God or a way to legitimize our ideas, I have news for you:

In this section, I will provide a brief synopsis of Dr. Ivan Panin's work but I encourage you to read further. Dr. Ivan Panin left Russia during the Bolshevik revolution and moved to the United States. He became a Harvard scholar, professor and mathematician. His life work was to scientifically prove the divine inspiration of Scripture. For fifty years, Dr. Panin spent twelve to eighteen hours a day devoted to his work. What was his work?

The Old Testament was written in Hebrew. The New Testament was written in Greek. The Hebrew and Greek languages use the letters of their alphabets as numbers. So the entire Bible is also written numerically. What Dr. Panin discovered is that the sixty-six books of the Bible show a pattern of numbers and divisibility that no other writings have. He diligently researched other Hebrew and Greek writings where he found no such pattern including the apocryphal books added in the Catholic Bible as well as other Protestant Bibles including the original King James version before its many revisions.

I mentioned that the number seven is by far the most common number used in the Bible. In Revelation, it is used more than fifty times but it is also common beneath the surface of the Bible text.

In the first verse in Genesis, there are seven Hebrew words. The total number of Hebrew letters in these seven words is twenty-eight, a multiple of seven. The number of letters in the first three words is fourteen (2x7). The last four Hebrew words consist of two objects, the heavens and the earth. The number of letters in the first object is seven. The number of letters in the second object is seven. The three leading words are 'God," the subject of the sentences, and 'heavens and earth,' the objects of the sentence. The number of letters in the three Hebrew words is fourteen (2x7). The number of letters in the remaining four words is fourteen (2x7). The shortest word is in the middle. The number of letters in the middle word plus and the word to the left of the middle word is seven. The number of letters in the middle word plus the word to the right is seven.

These number features are hidden beneath the surface of the text. They cannot be detected by the casual reader and are only discovered by intentionally searching the numerical structure of the original text. Dozens of other structures are found in this verse alone and Dr. Panin claims that the entire Bible is written this way!

The book of Matthew outlines the genealogy of Christ. The number of Greek vocabulary words in the first eleven verses is forty-nine (7x7). The number of letters in these forty-nine words in 266 (38x7). Out of these letters, the number of vowels is exactly 140 (20x7) and the number of consonants is 126 (18x7).

Out of these forty-nine words, there are twenty-eight words that begin with a vowel (4x7) and twenty-one words that begin with a consonant (3x7). Of those forty-nine words, forty-two (6x7) are nouns and seven are not nouns. Of the forty-two nouns, thirty-five (5x7) are proper nouns and seven are common nouns. In these seven common nouns, there are forty-nine (7x7) letters. The thirty-five proper nouns occur sixty-three (9x7) times. Of those proper nouns, twenty-eight (4x7) are male names and seven are not. The twenty-eight male names occur fifty-six (8x7) times.

Three women's names are mentioned in these first eleven verses: Tamar, Rahab and Ruth. The number of Greek letters in these three names is fourteen (2x7). Just one city is mentioned: Babylon and the number of Greek letters in Babylon is seven.

Of the forty-nine Greek vocabulary words that occur in the first eleven verses, there are thirty-five (5x7) words which appear more than once and fourteen (2x7) words which are used only once. There are forty-two (6x7) words which appear in one form and seven words which appear in more than one form (example, noun, verb, adjective).

You will never read the genealogy of Christ in the same way again. It holds more meaning than just the narrative histories of the Messiah's ancestors. Its very structure is inundated with patterns of seven no matter how it is dissected.

Further delving into these patterns of seven explores the probability of these numeric features to occur accidentally. For one feature, the chance of being an accident is one in seven. For twenty-four features to occur in the same passage, there is one chance in quintillions (million, billion, trillion, quadrillion, quintillion). Much of the research that Dr, Panin did shows that passages have up to seventy to one hundred features in the structure of the text. If this is not enough to convince you, he also found patterns not only of seven but simultaneous patterns of 8, 11, 13, 17, 19, 23, 37 and 43.

In the entire Bible, Moses is mentioned 847 (121x7) times. There are seven Old Testament writers mentioned in the New Testament: Moses, David, Isaiah, Jeremiah, Daniel, Hosea and Joel. These patterns can be used to detect errors and to connect book to book and the Old Testament to the New Testament.

This is not a trick or a scam. All this proves that One Divine brilliant mind wrote the Bible. The authors themselves were thirty-three simple men with relatively little education who lived in different countries and who wrote over a period of 1,600 years. It is impossible for them to have been aware of the numerical patterns in their writings and even if they had been, they each had to have been the last one to write their book.

In my Bible study group, we tried to write a sentence with only three numerical patterns. It was a challenge. Few succeeded and those who did created a meaningless sentence. The entire Bible is written this way. Computers can be programmed to follow certain patterns but the text they produce is incoherent as well. God accomplished this within stories, poetry, prophecy and with lists of genealogy.

Ancient Hebrew scribes followed strict rules when copying the manuscripts of Scripture. Since in Hebrew, letters are also numbers, each line and each page had to add up. If mistakes were made, the page was burned in the fire. This practice ensured that only correct copies were in existence. How do we know? If a letter or word is added, deleted or changed, it breaks the pattern in the text. God did this through the Hebrews to preserve the pattern of perfection in the Scriptures so that we could have the God-breathed Word of God.

Knowing this, other things in the Bible make sense that we might not have understood before. For example, Jesus said that not a jot nor a tittle should be changed until all is fulfilled. The book of Revelation warns sternly not to tamper with the words in the book or one who does will suffer plagues. The number of the antichrist is the number of a man and that number is 666.

This intricate system of patterns cannot be duplicated or denied by anyone. This is definitely not an accident. Drop a bag of eight oranges onto the floor and never in a million times would they arrange themselves into two even and straight rows of four. On the other hand, if you saw two lines of four oranges on the floor, you may come to a variety of conclusions but not, "someone dropped a bag of oranges."

Not only do the complex patterns prove that God wrote the Bible and that each word is from Him but, each word has meaning and is true. This shows a glimpse of who God is. He is brilliant. He is beyond us. We have seen it in nature and science. We have seen Him work in history. Now we see Him in language and math.

Whatever problems you are facing, whatever decisions you must make, whatever thoughts and feelings you have, whatever your life, culture, city, nation, God is sovereign. He is in control. There is nothing that He cannot accomplish. You can rely on Him.

Prayer

We fall down, we lay our crowns at the feet of Jesus.

_____

_____

_____

_____

_____

_____

36

will You come

We should live our lives as though Christ was coming this afternoon.

~ Jimmy Carter

God never made a promise that was too good to be true.

~ Dwight L. Moody

When I close my eyes
Will You still see me
And when I let go of Your hand
Will You still touch me
Can the song of the heavens
Still be heard when no one sings
And If I don't understand
Will You come
As You promised
When I am afraid
Can there still be joy
And when I am no longer brave
Can there still be love
Can You still redeem Your people
With the hope of a little boy
Can You still redeem Your people
When there's none to believe
And if I don't understand
Will You come
As You promised
Come to bring hope for those in darkness
And in death

It is Jesus
Jesus
Bringing Life
And when I
Don't understand
Will You Come

To what extent does God's plan depend on me? That's what I am asking. If I fail, will He still be faithful? Thankfully, the answer is that it does not depend on me. To what extent does it include me? Thankfully, it includes me to the fullest.

Isaiah 9:6

For to us a child is born,
*   to us a son is given,*
*   and the government will be on his shoulders.*
And he will be called
*   Wonderful Counsellor, Mighty God,*
*   Everlasting Father, Prince of Peace.*

Not and Ought

Do you remember the story of Shadrach, Meshach and Abednego? King Nebuchadnezzar of Babylon threw them into the fiery furnace for not bowing down to the huge image he set before them. And remember how God came into the furnace and rescued them and they weren't even singed? They did not even smell like smoke.

This story is not about them. It is not about great rescues or great healing. Actually, what's intriguing about Shadrach, Meshach and Abednego is what they said *before* going into the furnace: we know that God has the power to rescue us and save us from this horrible fate but even if He doesn't, we still won't bow to your image (Daniel 3:16-18).

"Even if He doesn't." What did they know about God that caused them to believe even if God didn't show up? Because sometimes, often, God doesn't show up. Do you believe me? He can do great things and He does, because He's God. But sometimes we pray for something deeply meaningful and nothing happens. People get sick, people get hurt, people die.

Michelangelo, the famous Italian sculptor and painter, said, "I saw the angel in the marble and carved until I set him free. Every block of stone has a statue inside it and it is the task of the sculptor to set it free."

Let's use his famous statue of David as an example. The concept is that David the perfect statue was already inside this block of marble. Michelangelo had to remove everything in the marble that was *not* David. Conversely, if you take everything that is *not* David, it will, by stark contrast, show us what *is* David. If we did not have David, the very existence of everything that is *not* David would testify to the existence of David.

For illustration, a clay mould works better than a sculpture. What if we call the statue David the Kingdom of God and we call everything that is *not* David the kingdom of men or the world as it is now.

In what is *not* the kingdom of God, we suffer greatly. We have loneliness, bullying, ridicule pain, families split apart, anger, what we call love fades away and disappears, we get sick, there are accidents, earthquakes, fires, diseases, people get hurt, get old, everyone dies . . .

But the *not* also tells us about what is the Kingdom of God. "They shall not hurt or destroy in all my holy mountain" (Isaiah 11:9). "The wolf will lie down with the lamb" (Isaiah 11:6). "He shall wipe away every tear from their eye" (Revelation 21:4). "And there shall be no death, neither grieving nor clamour, neither shall there be disease again nor pain" (Revelation 7:17).

So the *not* stands in contrast to what the *ought* will be. We live in the *not* and it hurts; it hurts when people get sick and die, it hurts when families fall apart, it hurts to live here. But we recognize the kingdom of God when we feel intensely the pain and suffering of the *not*.

Jesus healed the sick and cured diseases (some) and cleansed the lepers (some) and made blind people see (some not all) and restored people's lives (not many) and raised people from the dead (just a few) But he didn't do it for everyone. In Matthew 15:39 there were crowds of people to see him and Jesus told his disciples to get in a boat. His disciples advocated for the crowds who had come to be healed. They needed Jesus yet, Jesus got in a boat and left. What about about them? What about their needs? What about our needs?

Jesus is not a medicine cabinet. He came to show us that the world is *not* what it should be. He came to show us what it can be and what it will be through him.

When Jesus got the message that Lazarus, his close friend, was sick, he had time to return to Bethany and heal him. Instead, he did a strange thing: he did *not* show up. He waited until Lazarus was dead. When he showed up they said, "If you had been here he wouldn't have died."

But there was a purpose for Lazarus' death. By Lazarus' death, Jesus taught us the truth about resurrection. By Lazarus' death, Jesus taught us the truth about who he really is and where his power comes from.

So when you experience the suffering and hurt and pain and death of this kingdom of man, and you pray and it feels like God did *not* show up, please remember that the *not* is the proof of the "angel in the marble." The *not* stands in contrast to what the *ought* will be, that is, the Kingdom of God.

Prayer

Lord, will You come as You promised?

_____

_____

_____

_____

_____

_____

37

with His own arm

Like when you sit in front of a fire in winter — you are just there in front of the fire. You don't have to be smart or anything. The fire warms you.

~ Desmond Tutu

But the man who is not afraid to admit everything that he sees to be wrong with himself, and yet recognizes that he may be the object of God's love precisely because of his shortcomings, can begin to be sincere. His sincerity is based on confidence, not in his own illusions about himself, but in the endless, unfailing mercy of God.

~ Thomas Merton

God looked down
On a sinful people (Isaiah 59:16)
Saw they didn't know peace
Didn't know love
Didn't know Him
Not one turned an eye to heaven
There was no one to intervene (Isaiah 59:8)
With His own arm He established
Victory

God loved us so much
He didn't think twice to give
His only beloved son
That if we believe it
We will not walk in darkness
But we will have everlasting life (John 3:16)

Everything you are
And everything you see
Comes from God our Father (Psalm 24)
You are not your own
You were bought with a price
The price of Jesus God's son

Don't worry about your problems
He's got it under control (Romans 8:28)
Hear His call it'll work out
Keep turning your eyes to heaven (1Corinthians 6:20)
Follow the way of peace
You'll be a crown of beauty in His hand (Isaiah 60:3)

Any song, any style and any age: this is the message we have to share. Any Bible verse you want to study simply circles back to this theme. God saw there was a need. No one else could correct the problem. He solved it Himself. God, out of His love, put this plan into action. I don't understand the plan. I can't tell you why Jesus had to become a man and be hung on a cross or how, logically, his death atones for our problems. I just know that this is how God chose to express His love. And all the evidence points to the same person, Jesus. So, I accept it. If this is how He wants to do it, it behooves me to learn it and know it. Since God is big and powerful and actually the Creator of heaven and earth, planets and galaxies, the atom and subatomic particles, why would I question it? I'll do it. When my boss declares the new policy and explains my responsibility in it, I don't ignore it, deny it or question it. I do my job. God is much bigger than my boss. And I figure He knows what He is doing. Especially when every story, every action and every message says the same thing. It is no coincidence. Anyone looking for evidence has found it.

John 3:16

For God so loved the world that he gave his one and only Son, that whoever believes in him shall not perish but have eternal life

Join A Gym!

Last year, I joined a gym! I started exercising vigorously three to four times a week. I had been a runner in my youth but, since having kids, the demands of life made exercising sporadic at best and non-existent for long periods of time. So, I made the commitment last year after hitting rock bottom in frustration, lack of a feeling of control, anxiety, stress, diminishing energy . . . . you know.

It changed my life. You could say that I repented of my poor habits and because of my commitment, became a new person. Some of the benefits I've seen are: a levelling out of emotional fluctuations, disappearance of joint pain, increased cardio-vascular endurance, muscle gain, better management of my time and I spend less money buying superfluous (read: junk) food. And to top it off, people at the gym are so nice to me. Someone trained them well. When I arrive, they greet me and call me by name. They always speak to me when they walk past me by and never let me leave without calling my name and saying goodbye.

Well, that was a good testimony. Everything is true. I really believe in what I am doing and I'm excited about my experience, what it's doing for my life, and what the future holds for me.

What about you? Are you going to make the commitment to join a gym and exercise vigorously three to four times a week? I know what you are thinking: 'That's fine for you. I'm happy it's working for you but . . .' and the excuses flow: 'I don't have money to join a gym. I don't have time. My body won't do that stuff, my joints hurt, I have a bad heart, a bad back, I'm not consistent, it would never work.'

I wonder, when we share the testimony of our experience with God, if people have similar reactions, 'Great. I'm glad it's working for you but . . . .' They see obstacles and struggles that they can't get past in order to accept God in their lives.

I had an interesting conversation at school with a grade ten student. The class was working on a project using computers. This boy wanted to talk. He had some interesting things to say but I had to re-direct him to get back to work on his project. That's my job. Finally, some minutes before the bell, he returned. I was busily trying to finish my own work before dismissal. He took out his cell phone, pushed a few buttons slid his thumb around and read to me. "For God so loved the world that he gave his one and only Son, that whoever believes in him shall not perish but have eternal life" (John 3:16).

I smiled and carried on with my work as he read.

"Do you believe this?" he asked.

"Yes," I answered and carried on with my work.

"Then I am very insulted that you are not trying to convert me."

I put down my pen.

"And what must you think of all these people," he motioned around the room to the other kids in the class, "that you are not telling them about this?"

He had me. We talked.

He challenged me to convert him. I told him that I can't convert him. I am merely a post along the path of his journey.

"You can't convert me," he said, "but you can introduce me to your God."

That's the answer isn't it? I can't convince you to join a gym and exercise vigorously three to four times a week. I can't convince you to become a Christian and let God change your life and do for you all He has done for me. But I can tell you that God is real and that He comes to you in love and peace and with mounds of forgiveness and with a future full of promise.

God is going to do what He said He would do. He will accomplish it for you personally, if you want it, for our families and for our world. We have a choice. We can jump in or let Him drive on past.

There, I've introduced you.

Prayer

I want everyone to know this. No matter how long or how in-depth I study the Bible, this is the treasure I find. Every treasure is this treasure. It is the simplest thought; it is the deepest thought. It is our future hope. In the world to come, it will be our song of praise. And why wouldn't we be praising You, for we will have been dead and we will be alive only because of You. This is my prayer that everyone will know this.

_____

_____

_____

_____

_____

38

where does the wind go

When I lay these questions before God I get no answer. But a rather special sort of 'No answer.' It is not the locked door. It is more like a silent, certainly not uncompassionate, gaze. As though He shook His head not in refusal but waiving the question. Like, 'Peace, child; you don't understand."

~ C.S. Lewis

Prayer is always a privilege . . . a privilege to commune with the King of Kings and Lord of lords. ... remember this is ultimately a passage about God's grace rather than the "need" for human effort.

~ Michael Postlethwait

There's a room in my heart
With shelves lined with books
With books lined with words of my heart's desire
The words float like balloons
With every pulse of my heart
Every breath on my tongue flies with wings on the wind

But where does the wind go
Where does the time flow
Where do the cries go
Will we ever know
Where does the wind go
Where does the love flow
Where does a prayer go
Can I follow

There's a house full of pain
Where every room holds the rain
And in darkness contains
My heart's desire
Thought the curtain is drawn
It sways to respond
The rain finds where it belongs
To dance on the wind

But where does the wind go

Hearing the quiet sounds that are calling out to You
Concealing the secret things that are carried on the wind
Knowing the promises in my heart I know are true
Revealing the secret things that are carried on the wing
My heart will follow You

I will follow

It astounds me that people will give up on what they do not understand. Think high school math! I give up! That's it! I don't want anything more to do with it! As if math is just going to go away, disappear and never be part of my life again. In fact, it is everywhere! I cannot escape it. It lurks in the darkest corner. It creeps up and finds me in my daily routine: the grocery store, the restaurant, my household chores!

For thirty years, I have been running from math. I find myself exasperated. I should have listened to my father when he told me to learn my times tables in grade three!! Dad, you were right. It has followed me everywhere! But, like the parable of the Rich Man and Lazarus (Luke 16:19-31), by the time he understood, it was too late.

Jeremiah 33:3

Call to me and I will answer you and tell you great and unsearchable things you do not know.

Wind

Who has seen the wind? Where does the wind go? What causes wind? All very good questions to inspire poetry.

The wind is invisible. What is visible are the effects of wind in nature; both strong powerful winds and gentle breezes. Where does it go? To know that you must know where it comes from. What causes wind? Mainly two things: the difference in temperature of the air and therefore, air pressure. Air moves from high pressure to low pressure areas. And secondly, our planet rotates so the air is deflected by the Coriolis effect (except exactly at the equator).

The wind, then, is the result of constant motion on a grand scale. So much for poetry. Human relationship with the wind is complicated. It is refreshing when a warm, spring wind brushes through your hair or a cool breeze urges your sail on a lake during summer vacation. Then, of course, the wind is beneficial for sailing ships and hot air balloons, aircraft used for travel, surveillance and war. Sometimes strong winds retaliate: scatter meticulously-placed items, send animals into hiding, damage trees and destroy buildings. Unseen and ubiquitous, the wind moves us, aids us, stirs us to respond.

So, too, the Spirit of God who is the wind. In Hebrew, the word for Spirit is "re-ach" which literally means breath or wind. We can see the same roots in our English word. Think of words like inspiration, respiration have to do with breathing and breathing is moving the air to continue to give us life.

Prayer

Dear God, may this be an ongoing thing, prayer. May we always turn to You and find our answers in You.

_____

_____

_____

_____

_____

_____

39

you can pray

What a friend we have in Jesus, all our sins and griefs to bear.
What a privilege to carry everything to God in prayer.

~ Joseph Scriven

Where there is great love there are always miracles.

~ Willa Cather

It's a quiet night where dreams go unheard
As the city home fires twinkle across the land
It's a dreamer's night and screams go unheard
Beneath the rumble creeping devastation that tears us apart

It's clear now there's nothing I can do
I'm powerless motionless and so afraid
But every dreamer eventually awakens
And every name can be whispered to convince you it's the right thing to do

But you can pray
And believe you are right where you need to be
You can pray
And believe He will use you to brighten the blackest of nights

The sky's a mirror suspended in space
Reflecting every movement on the ground
There's a fog in the valley and stars in the sky
But above all this my petition is to see them sparkle in your eyes

But you can pray

And believe you are right where you need to be

You can pray

And believe He will use you to brighten the blackest of nights

But if you do nothing; sit quietly in your corner

Admiring what hangs on your walls

At best I can stand it does me no good

But if I take your hand I know it would

Replace the gloom around us,

The wave that wants to drown us

With the Hand that waits to guides us

Though I dare not speak His Name

According to Moses, God said in Deuteronomy 25:4, "Do not muzzle an ox while it is treading out the grain," In 1 Corinthians 9:9, Paul uses this law as an example to make a point. Paul asks, "Is it about oxen that God is concerned? Surely he says this for us, doesn't he?" So what's the lesson about muzzling an ox? While this ox is doing work for you, don't deprive him of eating. Be tender-hearted. Don't be thoughtless (which is unintentional). Don't be mean (which is deliberate).

We are instructed to pray: to talk to God freely about our thoughts, feelings and experiences. And we are also to pray for other people. Jesus was our great example as he lived his life connected to God in prayer. He prayed for people he was with and he even prayed for us down the corridor of time (John 17).

Did God tell us to pray so that He could find out what is going in our lives and in our hearts? No. He already knows all of that. And when He encourages us to pray for others is it because He wants to know their business? No. My guess is that He tells us to talk to Him because of the effect it has on us. He asks us to pray for others even when He knows their needs and even when He has already been working in their lives. Why? Because prayer affects not only the one who is prayed for but also the one who prays. It creates loving people. It turns our thoughts away from ourselves and our own problems. Prayer develops a love for others.

Esther 4:14

For if you remain silent at this time, relief and deliverance for the Jews will arise from another place, but you and your father's family will perish. And who knows but that you have come to your royal position for such time as this?

Puzzle Piece

This verse succinctly illustrates the idea that God does not need us to pray in order to fulfill His will on this planet. The Bible clearly and repeatedly confirms that God will do what He said He will do. In the story of Esther, Mordecai was correct in concluding that God would save the Jews by another means if Esther did not participate. In her situation, she had the privilege of being a vehicle for God to save them.

How did it affect her? The first time she invited Haman and the King to her banquet, she was petrified by fear. She failed to bring her request to the King and to expose Haman and his plot. It took a second try. God is sovereign. He even weaves our weaknesses into His plan. You see, the gallows were not ready when Esther first entertained Haman and the king.

This was a growth experience for Esther. It strengthened her resolve. Mordecai was somehow able to see God's plan. In convincing Esther to pray, he placed her in God's hands. Mordecai placed her in God's active hands for God to do something with her. God achieved His purposes that day when Esther surrendered to Him for good or for ill. "If I perish, I perish." Mordecai knew that she had been placed in the position of Queen for just this situation.

Perhaps it's clear to you how God is moving you around like a chess piece to accomplish His purpose. Perhaps you and I may need to wait for the day the "books are opened" to fully understand how our saying this or moving here, though seemingly insignificant, was in fact an essential part of God's plan. Like a piece of a jigsaw puzzle, small, insignificant and scarcely identifiable on its own, suddenly brings the entire puzzle to its completion when simply secured in its rightful place.

Prayer

Father, I will accept that challenge and remember to pray for others. Not because You need reminders but exactly because I need to be reminded to care

_____

_____

_____

_____

_____

_____

40

you thought of me

I love to think of nature as an unlimited broadcasting station, through which God speaks to us every hour, if we will only tune in.

~ George Washington Carver

The human brain is ' ... the most complex and orderly arrangement of matter in the universe'.

~ Isaac Asimov

A tiny seed embedded in the centre of a pear
So minuscule and silent you don't even know it's there
It holds the information that can fill a library
That tiny seed knows how to turn itself into a tree
And it brings me to my knees

My bones my skin, my muscles, my thoughts and my dear heart
I move I laugh, I hurt I cry I understand in part
When the sceptics ask, "Where is this God? How can we know He's true?"
How can I deny the masterpiece of everything You do
And it brings me to my knees

To know You thought of me
You sculpted me
You breathed Your life in me
I am the evidence, the consequence
The love reality
And it brings me to my knees
When I think of what You made
I can see, I can see Your love for me.

There's more to this creation
Than winding up and letting go
Go has stated His commitment
And He tries to let us know

Once in the mall, someone holding a clipboard asked me to give ten minutes of my time for a survey. They walked me down a hall and showed me a 15-second video commercial about a candy bar. Having never tasted that particular type, I did my best to answer their questions. Then they showed me another video about the same candy bar and asked me some more questions. For the third time, they showed me a video and asked me questions. They thanked me for my time and sent me on my way.

You have to understand the gravity of what I am about to tell you. This was a time in my life when I lived in a health-conscious community and I had made a commitment to healthy living. I was young and had no spending money. But, for the next two weeks, every time I went to a store, I bought a that type of candy bar. I don't even like that particular one.

Before watching those videos, I didn't even know this candy bar existed. After my encounter and exposure to it, notwithstanding whatever psychological voo doo they did on me, it changed something in my brain and it changed my behaviour. I can extrapolate that if I were to watch the same video once a week, I would probably continue to embrace and promote that candy bar.

This is a trite comparison but when you encounter God, when you inundate yourself in His Presence and His word, it bends you. It affects your faith, your perspective of the world and it changes the way you relate to people. It changes the way you understand God and His role in our lives and on the planet. *Turn your eyes upon Jesus. Look full in his wonderful face. And the things of earth will grow strangely dim in the light of his glory and grace.*

Psalm 139:14

I praise you because I am fearfully and wonderfully made; Your works are wonderful. I know that full well.

I'm a Genius!

The other day, I wrote a wonderful letter and I had to mail it. I didn't want to fold it up and put a stamp on my important letter. I discovered this: An envelope. What happens when I put the paper inside the envelop? It fits perfectly! It's a miracle!!!

Later, I wanted to tidy up the kitchen drawers. I have measuring cups all over the place. They are all different colours and sizes and they take up so much room in my drawers. But, I discovered that they stack one inside the other so they don't take up so much room in my drawer. It's a miracle. Maybe not. Maybe it's just an accident, a coincidence.

Wait, one more thing to show my genius: Have you ever played catch with a baseball? If you play with someone who throws hard, what happens when you catch the ball? Ouch. I made another discovery that I want to share with you. There is what they call a baseball glove and it helps you catch the ball by being just the right size to hold a baseball. I'm a genius. It's a miracle. No? It's not? Then it must be an accident. A coincidence.

Does it sound ridiculous to reason this way, to take the credit for the discovery or to ignore that someone designed it to fit a specific purpose?

Think of a woodpecker: What do woodpeckers do that other birds don't do? They bang their head against a tree. Do they ever get dizzy? Do they hurt themselves when they bang continually on a tree? They have little shock absorbers in their head behind their beak so that they don't get hurt. There is something to buffer the pounding so that they can do what they have to do to find food in the tree. How long would I have to bang my head against a tree before I developed shock absorbers?

It's a miracle. Oh no it's not. It's an accident? No. Somebody thought of and designed it. Who did? God did. He's a genius.

Another example of God's genius is the structure of the eye. Do you realize that you can see? Have you ever wondered how you can see? To explain how we see, scientists talk about light and lenses and cones and rods. A camera can duplicate the effect of light and how it is captured. That's amazing in itself. Like the ball and glove, like the letter and the envelop, it fits together.

But the eye mechanism with its lenses and cones and rods sends that message through the optic nerve to the brain. And the brain has just the right receptors to make sense of the information and, voilà, without effort, you can see. Scientists try to duplicate it but they cannot. They can do what the eye can do but they cannot do what the brain can do.

There's more. For instance, your brain is designed to compensate for movement so that when your eye moves, the world does not. A camera can't do that. Try it. Roll your eyes around. The world stays still as you move. Now gently touch your eye at the side and move your eyeball. The world moves.

It's a miracle. No, it's not. Well, it's not an accident. It's a masterpiece! Someone designed it. It was someone's idea. Whose? Our Creator God's. Now that's genius!

Prayer

How can we do anything but marvel? You are so beyond us. The more we learn, the more we learn about You. Even our very cells are intricately designed to function in ways that keep us alive. They do that without our knowledge for the most part and without our participation yet, they still function. Our heart still beats and we keep breathing because You have made things to function and fit. I offer you my puny thanks.

_____

_____

_____

_____

_____

_____

conclusion

The world does not consist of 100 percent Christians and 100 percent non-Christians. There are people (a great many of them) who are slowly ceasing to be Christians but who still call themselves by that name: some of them are clergymen. There are other people who are slowly becoming Christians though they do not yet call themselves so.

~ C.S. Lewis

Conversion is a daily thing.

~ Jim Caviezel

When I thought that the Bible was a collection of stories that revealed, in metaphor, unfathomable secrets of God, it was understandable to treat it like 'just another way to God' or to make room for other beliefs along side of it. We are all looking for God, aren't we? Now I see how God communicates with us. He has had the same plan from the beginning, the same message through time; I understand that He has woven Himself into our history and embedded Himself into the Bible.

It sounds ludicrous to me that I should need a conversion. I was one who searched the Bible and longed for God. After all my years of Bible study and fervent longing for God, I was in need of conversion. At the time, it seemed right what I was doing, and objectively, it was. But, once my eyes saw God and I realized who Jesus is, all of that 'scholarship' and striving changed. In fact, I needed to repent not of particular wrongdoing but to acknowledge that this is not a fantasy, a mystery or a game, a hobby, a duty or an expertise. God is real. He loves us and He has a plan for this world. And He has been, has loved and has had all along.

The irony is that what I am writing is not new. It has been shouted from the hilltops and whispered in the wind for centuries. I've known it all my life but I only thought I understood. I feel the need to write because I have a new perspective from which I see what I have always seen. It's like looking at the garden all day long. It's a garden. You weed it, water it, sit in it, read beside it, absorb all the benefits all day long. Then, in the evening as the sun descends, the garden is covered in golden light and every flower, every leaf, every stray twig and even the weeds are bathed in a newness. The garden shimmers with life and joy.

If it's just a story, then Jesus was just a guy. He taught us values to treat each other right. Jesus spoke against religious leaders and educated scholars who had a choke hold on their society. Jesus wants us to love God, love each other. None of this is false. But, if Jesus is real, what I mean is, if God is real and if the Bible is real, then everything transfigures. It all changes. It stays exactly the same, like the garden. The garden did not move or change but it transfigured.

I used to believe that religion and the Bible were a shroud around the truth. I believed that I was smart enough and strong enough to expose the deceit of organized religion and to discover the truth. I used to believe that the truth would set me free from the false hope that others held to help them through life. I believed that I would have a realistic view of God that made sense according to modern physics, one that would coincide with our social issues, one that could be fit comfortably into our modern ideas.

I used to believe I could evaluate God's decrees and confirm or deny His stipulations. That statement, of itself, dilutes the notion of an Almighty, all-knowing God and it places me above Him. It is ridiculous to put oneself above God, yet we make this common mistake when we impose our own ideas of who God is and what He is doing.

When I finally understood what I have heard all my life, that God wrote the Bible, that the Bible is sacred and is indeed His message to us, it changed everything. The closest I can come to describe what I experienced is repentance. I abandoned my position of judge and jury over the Bible. I laid down my weapons of scholarly critical thinking, analysis and evaluation of the stories, themes audiences, purposes, turns of phrase. I submitted, relented and accepted that God is real not just an amusing, intellectual exercise. Like a Pharisee and a Priest, I was content in the system. I lived and breathed in a system that worked for me. A system that put me in the centre. A system that had me as god.

All who read the gospels know that Jesus was kind and compassionate to people especially those in need. He loved them, taught them and healed them. He was stern, challenging and demanding of his disciples. He taught them, brought them into a deeper understanding of God and His plan and he had high expectations of them. But, it is obvious to the point of embarrassment and it cannot be ignored that Jesus could not tolerate the religious powers of his nation: *the priests* who were in charge of the Temple and the Temple services (which were representative in a perfect Jungian way of God's love and plan for humanity), *the pharisees* who taught the law and were guardians of the culture of the Jewish nation (the law is a representation of the character and heart of God) and *the scribes*, who wrote out the sacred words, in whose hands was passed down the marvellous miracle that God preserved in writing, to speak to multiple nations and generations.

The Jews had been entrusted out of all the nations of people on the planet, with the football. Their job is to carry it to the goal post, to get the touch down, to run with the ball until the end. When Jesus walked the earth, they had long dropped the ball and were running with a tattered replacement.

If you know the promises from Genesis, the promises God made to Abraham and the promises to David that God revealed to the Jewish prophets, the timeline of history that we know in retrospect, that they saw laid out before them, then you know that Jesus' arrival was planned, prophesied and pre-ordained. But, the entire Jewish nation was oblivious to Jesus. Imagine a wedding reception where guests are so preoccupied with their own personal dramas that no one notices when the bride and groom enter. They did not recognize Jesus. Even that was foretold. However, the foretelling and the foreknowledge does not lessen the emotional impact of rejection. You can be warned your partner is going to break up with you but the process hurts just the same. Because of their leaders, the entire nation missed the one grand thing they had been waiting for. He came and lived among them and they did not recognize him (John 1:10).

If this is just a story, we learn it, take a lesson from it and move on with our lives. But if God is real and His love for us is real and His plan (which is Jesus) is real, then this is serious.

To a handful of people, Jesus was the Messiah promised of God. To the majority of people and those with decision-making power, he was a nuisance, then a threat and then a problem that needed to be eliminated. Why? Because they thought he was just another guy: just one of many troublemakers, just one of many teachers promoting one of many stories to give us hope. They thought they knew the scriptures but they stood as judge and jury over the words of God, over the Son of God. They put themselves in the centre. They were in a system that had them as god. God is real and Jesus is real. God had entrusted the most valuable thing on the planet, to these guys and they dropped the ball. They did not recognize him.

Repentance is when bad people change and become good. When the drug addict gives up his addiction. When the drunkard sheds his drunkenness. When the thief returns what he's stolen. When evil becomes good.

Maybe.

My story is different. Slightly.

Repentance.

Repentance is also when good people see God.

Jehovah God has kept His word. He is keeping His word. He will keep His word. Who was and who is and who will be. He is faithful and true. And to see Him, even a tiny glimpse of Him, is life changing.

appendix a

from Cyrano de Bergerac by Edmond Rostand

DE GUICHE:
   Will no one put him down?. . .

THE VISCOUNT:
   No one? But wait!
   I'll treat him to. . .one of my quips!. . .See here!. . .
(He goes up to Cyrano, who is watching him, and with a conceited air):
   Sir, your nose is. . .hmm. . .it is. . .very big!

CYRANO (gravely):
   Very!

THE VISCOUNT (laughing):
   Ha!

CYRANO (imperturbably):
   Is that all?. . .

THE VISCOUNT:
   What do you mean?

CYRANO:
   Ah no! young blade! That was a trifle short!
   You might have said at least a hundred things
   By varying the tone. . .like this, suppose,. . .
   Aggressive: 'Sir, if I had such a nose
   I'd amputate it!' Friendly: 'When you sup
   It must annoy you, dipping in your cup;
   You need a drinking-bowl of special shape!'
   Descriptive: "Tis a rock!. . .a peak!. . .a cape!

—A cape, forsooth! 'Tis a peninsular!'
   Curious: 'How serves that oblong capsular?
   For scissor-sheath? Or pot to hold your ink?'
   Gracious: 'You love the little birds, I think?
   I see you've managed with a fond research
   To find their tiny claws a roomy perch!'
   Truculent: 'When you smoke your pipe. . .suppose
   That the tobacco-smoke spouts from your nose—
   Do not the neighbors, as the fumes rise higher,
   Cry terror-struck: "The chimney is afire"?'
   Considerate: 'Take care,. . .your head bowed low
   By such a weight. . .lest head o'er heels you go!'
   Tender: 'Pray get a small umbrella made,
   Lest its bright color in the sun should fade!'
   Pedantic: 'That beast Aristophanes
   Names Hippocamelelephantoles
   Must have possessed just such a solid lump
   Of flesh and bone, beneath his forehead's bump!'
   Cavalier: 'The last fashion, friend, that hook?
   To hang your hat on? 'Tis a useful crook!'
   Emphatic: 'No wind, O majestic nose,
   Can give THEE cold!—save when the mistral blows!'
   Dramatic: 'When it bleeds, what a Red Sea!'
   Admiring: 'Sign for a perfumery!'
   Lyric: 'Is this a conch?. . .a Triton you?'
   Simple: 'When is the monument on view?'
   Rustic: 'That thing a nose? Marry-come-up!
   'Tis a dwarf pumpkin, or a prize turnip!'
   Military: 'Point against cavalry!'
   Practical: 'Put it in a lottery!
   Assuredly 'twould be the biggest prize!'
   Or. . .parodying Pyramus' sighs. . .
   'Behold the nose that mars the harmony
   Of its master's phiz! blushing its treachery!'
—Such, my dear sir, is what you might have said,
   Had you of wit or letters the least jot:
   But, O most lamentable man!—of wit

You never had an atom, and of letters
You have three letters only!—they spell Ass!
And—had you had the necessary wit,
To serve me all the pleasantries I quote
Before this noble audience. . .e'en so,
You would not have been let to utter one—
Nay, not the half or quarter of such jest!
I take them from myself all in good part,
But not from any other man that breathe

appendix b

ten plagues: Jehovah versus the gods of egypt

	Plague	Egyptian gods	Notes
1	water turned to blood Exodus 7: 14-25	Khnum guardian of the river's source Hapi spirit of the Nile Osiris Nile was his bloodstream	duplicated by the Egyptians occurred in Goshen dead fish; putrid smell
2	frogs Exodus 8:1-15	Hapi frog goddess to Egypt Heqt both related to fertility	duplicated by the Egyptians occurred in Goshen where Israelites lived
3	lice Exodus 8:16-19	Seb the earth god	not duplicated by the Egyptians occurred in Goshen attributed to the finger of God
4	flies Exodus 8:20-22	Uatchit the fly god	God now makes a separation between the Egyptians and the Israelites No more plagues on the Israelites
5	disease on the cattle Exodus 9:1-7	Ptah Mnevis gods associated with Hathor Amon bulls and cows	affects property death of livestock
6	boils Exodus 9:8-12	Sekhmet goddess of epidemics Serapis gods of healing Imhotep	affects physical bodies Pharaoh's magicians cannot even appear in court
7	hail Exodus 9:13-35	Nut sky goddess Isis Seth agricultural deities Shu god of the atmosphere	historical uniqueness for such a storm in Egypt Pharaoh confesses but later changes his mind
8	locusts Exodus 10:1-20	Serapia protector from locusts	Pharaoh offers a compromise compromise is rejected Pharaoh again confesses his sin
9	darkness Exodus 10:21-29	Re, Amon-re, Aten, Atum, Horus : sun gods Thoth: moon god	dark at midday light provided for the Israelites in Goshen
10	death of the firstborn Exodus 12:39-46	This plague was a judgement on all Egypt's gods including Pharaoh	Pharaoh will now let Israel go.

appendix c
the feasts of the LORD

	activities and times	Jesus' life and movements
Nisan 9	Passover lambs are brought through the Northern Gate of the Temple. Psalm 118. Hosanna!	Jesus came through the Eastern Gate at the same time. People shouted Hosanna to him!
Nisan 10	Instructions were to take the passover lamb and hold it for four days.	From Adam to Christ is 4,000 years. The "lamb" was held for 4 days (a day is like a thousand years to God. Psalm 90:4, 2 Peter 3:8).
Nisan 10	Lambs were inspected. They had to be without blemish.	Jesus was interrogated for four days. They found no fault in him.
	The Passover lamb must be roasted, eaten with bitter herbs and unleavened bread and thrown in the fire.	Jesus was the burnt offering, sacrifice without sin, bitter experience and the fire represents his offering.
Passover Seder **Nisan 14**	Four cups to remember their plight in Egypt sanctification deliverance redemption acceptance	Through Christ we are sanctified, freed from the bondage of sin delivered and rescued from death redeemed, Jesus paid the price accepted by God as the perfect sacrifice.
Seder	Matzah striped and pierced there are three pieces: take out the middle one, break it, put it in a linen bag called the Afikomen and hide it. At the drinking of the third cup, it is found. Afikomen means, "I came."	Jesus was pierced for our iniquities and by his stripes we are healed (Isaiah 53:5) The Father, Son and Holy Spirit. He is in the middle. He died and was buried and on the third day rose as our redemption. This message couldn't be any clearer. He is shouting, "I came!"
Seder	Songs sung: Hallel The last him is Psalm 118 "You have become my salvation."	Yeshua has become our salvation.
	Bind the sacrifice with cords on the altar on the 3rd hour (9:00am) the time of the morning sacrifice.	The very hour they were binding the lamb to the altar, they were binding Jesus to the cross.
	Time of the evening sacrifice, 9th hour (3:00pm), the priest slew the passover lamb and said, "It is finished." Passover is over.	The very moment the priest slew the passover lamb, Jesus said, "It is finished" and died.
Unleavened Bread **Nisan 15**	Children help the father get all of the leaven out of the house before the feast of Unleavened Bread. Eat unleavened bread for 7 days.	Jesus turned over the tables in the Temple before passover helping his Father get the 'leaven' out of His house.

	activities and times	Jesus' life and movements
	The father takes a candle and a feather. The children look for hidden leaven. He sweeps the leaven onto a wooden spoon with a feather and wraps it in a linen cloth. He throws it outside in a communal bonfire.	Candle= word of God (Ps 119:105) feather= Spirit (Ps 91:4) leaven= sin (2 Cor 5:21) wooden spoon= the cross (Deut 21) linen cloth= shroud (Mark 15:46) fire= sacrificial offering (Hebrews 13:13)
Unleavened Bread **Nisan 15**	First day of the Feast of Unleavened bread commemorates the day Egypt buried its first born (Psalm 16:10).	The Father buried His firstborn in the grave.
First Fruits **Nisan 18**	According to Leviticus 23:10, 11 the day after the Sabbath is the barley harvest.	Sunday morning was Jesus' resurrection.
	At dawn, the priest waves the first sheaf (omer) of the harvest that is to come.	Christ became the first fruit of the resurrection at the very moment the priest is waving the first fruits of the barley harvest (Matthew 27:51, 52). Jesus is the first fruit of the resurrection to come.
+ 50 days **Pentecost**	Fifty days after the passover in Egypt was the giving of the law on Mount Sinai where 3,000 people died.	Fifty days after Jesus' sacrifice was the giving of the Spirit on the day of Pentecost where 3,000 people were saved.
	Counting the days of omer are for spiritual introspection and remembrance of the journey from Egypt to Sinai.	As they were counting the days, Jesus appeared to people. Jesus ascended on the 40th day (Acts 1:9).
	At Pentecost was the wheat harvest feast. There were 2.5 million people gathered in Jerusalem. They were instructed to attend.	They were all together because they had been commanded to be in Jerusalem three times a year (Deut 16:16) at Passover, Pentecost and the Feast of Tabernacles (or Booths).

appendix d
blood clotting process

There are processes, plans for things to function in our body, that are in place yet may never be used. Some get called on more frequently than others. A process that we do rely on almost daily is the systems that are in place, ready and waiting for blood clotting and healing of a wound.

We pay little attention to a small scratch or a cut that stops bleeding immediately. In fact, as long as it doesn't hurt, it can be easily ignored. It is taken for granted that it will stop bleeding.

But a blood clot must form to stop the bleeding. A clot must form in the right place and not stop the blood flow to critical areas. It must form at the right time. It must be strong and well-anchored.

The process of blood clotting is like a row of falling dominoes. It is a series of events that lead to the desired end. Knowing the complexity of the process makes us aware that we are designed, created and maintained by someone who loves us. You don't need to understand it, be able to follow it or remember how it works for it to work immediately on cue the next time you get cut.

The process involves names like: fibrinogen, thrombin, accelerin, proaccelerin, glutamate residues and kallidrem. I am going to simplify.

When an animal is cut,

- protein A sticks to the surface of cells near the wound
- another protein B comes to activate protein A
- the activated A converts another protein C to its active form
- protein C helps A to speed up to its activated form
- activated A and B together transform another protein D to its activated form
- activated D together with activated E switch another protein F to activated
- finally, activated F together with G changes H to its activated form and the blood stops.

But wait, once the blood stops flowing the healing begins. The growth of new cells is under tight control. The right kinds of cells and the right number needed must be produced. The cells must unite to form the same tissue of the same shape as required by the cut or wound.

This process is poised and waiting until the next time you injure yourself. We were formed by a wonderful mind and loving hands.

appendix e

Parallels between Joseph and Jesus

	Joseph	Jesus
first born	Genesis 30:22-24 (of Rachel)	Matthew 1:25 (of Mary)
shepherds	Genesis 37:2	Matthew 2:26, 26:31, John 10:11
prophesied to be rulers	Genesis 37:5-11	Daniel 7:13-14, Micah 4:7, 5:2, Psalm 2
most loved by their fathers	Genesis 37:3	Matthew 3:17, 12:18
brothers were jealous of him	Genesis 37:4-5, 11	John 7:3-5, 15:18-19
scheme to kill him to be rid of him	Genesis 37:18-28	Acts 2:22-23
sold for the price of a slave	Genesis 37:26-28	Matthew 26:15, Exodus 21:32, Zechariah 11:12-13
falsely accused	Genesis 39:11-20	Matthew 26:59-61
with two others condemned to die, one of which was pardoned	Genesis 40:1-3,20-22	Luke 23:32,39-43
God's Spirit dealt within	Genesis 41:38	Luke 4:1, Acts 10:38
exalted as ruler over all	Genesis 41:40-44	Acts 2:32-33, 1 Cor. 15:27-28
all knees will bow	Genesis 41:43	Philippians 2:10
seven years of tribulation	Genesis 41:54-55	Mark 13:8, Jeremiah 30:7
not recognized by own people	Genesis 42:8	John 1:10
finally revealed	Genesis 45:3	Zechariah 12:10, Matthew 24:30-31, Revelation 1:7
God used intended evil to save them (people)	Genesis 45:5-8, Genesis 50:20	Acts 3:12-18
therefore they are forgiven	Genesis 45:5,10-15	Luke 23:34
saviour	Genesis 47:25	Acts 13:23
sinless	(silent)	1 Peter 2:22

references

2. a flower bent

Feast of Tabernacles: Biltz, Mark. <u>*The Feasts of the Lord* Study Guide and Notes</u>. Bonney Lake: El Shaddai Ministries, 2008.

3. all my longing

carbon monoxide: Starr, Cecie and Taggart, Ralph. <u>Biology, the Unity and Diversity of Life</u>. Belmont, California: Wadsworth Publishing Company, 1981.

4. a thousand singing birds

neural pathways in the brain: Delude, Cathryn M. MIT News. Massachusetts Institute of Technology, October 19, 2005, (<u>http://news.mit.edu/2005/habit</u>).

feasts are dress rehearsals: Biltz, Mark. <u>The Feasts of the Lord.</u> Bonney Lake, WA: El Shaddai Ministries, 2008.

5. a whispered rescue

entropy: <u>*https://www.meriam-webster.com/dictionary/entropy*</u>

7. barely audible

the promised regathering in order: Schnittger, David, Dr. <u>Zechariah: Israel and Her Coming King.</u> Middletown, DE: Southwest Prophecy Ministries, 2018.

story about morse code: True Story On Morse Code, August 5, 2013 (<u>http://www.eham.net/ehamforum/smf/index.php/topic,91416.0.html</u>)

9. darkness into light

sun, moon, light: The Sun Our Source of Light and Life, March 10, 2011 (http://yellowmagpie.com/the-sun-our-source-of-light-and-life/).

why Jesus rebuked them: Major Herbert Sharp. *Open the Eyes of My Heart* (sermon). The Salvation Army, Peterborough Temple, Peterborough, Ontario. April 1, 2018.

10. daughters of Jerusalem

provide wine: Maurice Lamm. *Wine,* chabad.org (https://www.chabad.org/library/article_cdo/aid/481775/jewish/Wine.htm)

11. everybody but the bride

Jewish wedding: Glenn Kay. *Jewish Wedding Customs and the Bride of Messiah.* Grafted In Ministries, 2010. (http://www.messianicfellowship.50webs.com/wedding.html).

Ancient Jewish Wedding Customs and Yeshua's Second Coming. Bibles for Israel, 2018. (http://frec.messianicbible.com/feature/ancient-jewish-wedding-customs-and-yeshuas-second-coming/).

12. gettin' down hope

Daniel and the magi: Tom Stewart, *The Magi and The Star of Bethlehem*, December 2, 2002. (http://www.whatsaiththescripture.com/Fellowship/Edit_Magi_and_the_Star.html).

Nebuchadneszzar's "test": Missler, Dr. Chuck. Learn The Bible In 24 Hours. Nashville: Thomas Nelson, 2002.

13. goin' my way

Jesus was most influential in history: The Top Ten, *Jesus Christ,* 2018 (http://www.whatsaiththescripture.com/Fellowship/Edit_Magi_and_the_Star.html)

Jeff Struecker, *Why Jesus is still the most influential man in human history- even 2000 years after his death.* Calvary Baptist Church Columbus. Georgia. (https://calvaryga.com/jesus-still-influential-man-human-history-even-2000-years-death/)

well-versed in the literature of the Bible: Frye, Northrop. <u>The Great Code</u>. New York: Harcourt Brace Jovanovich Publishers,1982.

15. hidden jewel

genealogy: Chuck Missler. *Treasures in the Family Trees.* May 1, 2004. (http://www.khouse.org/articles/2004/522/).

16. hosea's love

I Know A Fount: Hymn by Oliver Cooke (20th century)

17. i love your kindness

lighthouse and the ship: The Lighthouse Joke, December 2, 2009. Washington D.C. (http://www.navy.mil/navydata/nav_legacy.asp?id=174).

21. lightning

Joseph's name: Blum, Julia. Israel Biblical studies.com. eTeacher Ltd. Ramat Gan, Israel, 2017.

Son of God Son of Man: Boyarin, Daniel. <u>The Jewish Gospels. The Story of the Jewish Christ.</u> New York: The New Press, 2012.

Ben Gurion's claim was the Bible: http://mondoweiss.net/2012/09/netanyahu-tells-a-christian-zionist-pal-that-the-bible-was-ben-gurions-claim-to-the-land/).

22. l'ombra dell' passato

ATP ADP: Starr, Cecie and Taggart, Ralph. <u>Biology, the Unity and Diversity of Life.</u> Belmont, California: Wadsworth Publishing Company, 1981.

24. meaning of my silence

Frye, Northrop. <u>Words With Power.</u> Markham, ON: Viking Press. 1990.

Rostand, Edmond. <u>Cyrano de Bergerac</u>. London: Heinemann Educational Books Ltd., 1962.

25. no one like you

Tozer, Aiden Wilson. <u>Knowledge of the Holy</u>. "Men may flee from the sunlight to dark and musty caves of the earth but they cannot put out the sun. So men in any dispensation despise the grace of God, but they cannot extinguish it." A.W. Tozer (1897 –1963).

ten plagues and the gods of Egypt:
https://i.pinimg.com/736x/5e/67/7b/5e677bf64e5347dde6fef1598c5eb2ec.jpg

the Feasts of the LORD: <u>http://www.hebrew4christians.com/Holidays/Introduction.html</u>

28. only in a song

Abraham: Whiston, William, A.M. <u>Josephus The Complete Works</u>. Nashville: Thomas Nelson Publishers, 1998.

29. prince of peace

quotations: Vladimir Putin (Jan 21, 2001 Moscow Times) and Mitsuo Fuchida (Japanese Navy Captain, April 1950).

30. secrets

blood clotting: Linda Crampton. How Blood Clots: Platelets and the Coagulation Cascade. June 27, 2017. (<u>https://owlcation.com/stem/How-Does-Blood-Clot-and-What-Causes-Coagulation</u>)

thrombocyte: *Ten Step Process of Blood Coagulation.* 2018. (<u>http://www.thrombocyte.com/process-of-blood-coagulation/</u>)

four fundamental forces: <u>http://hyperphysics.phy-astr.gsu.edu/hbase/Forces/funfor.html.</u>

31. send the rain away

paramonasia: James Bent Coffman
https://www.studylight.org/commentaries/bcc/isaiah-5.html.

33. struggle to believe

infinity between the numbers: Natalie Wolchover. *Dispute Over Infinity Divides Mathematicians.* Quanta Magazine. December 3, 2013. https://www.scientificamerican.com/article/infinity-logic-law/

35. who will listen

numerics Dr. Ivan Panin: Panin, Ivan. Panin's Bible Chronology In Three Parts. Sidney, ME: New England Bible Sales, 2014.

36. will You come

angel in the marble: Dustin Staiger, Angels in the Marble. The People Brand. June 21, 2013. (http://www.thepeoplebrand.com/blog/2013/06/21/angels-in-the-marble/).

not and ought: Tozer, A.W. The Knowledge of the Holy. Lexington, Kentucky, 2018

bibliography

Biltz, Mark. (2008). <u>The Feasts of the Lord</u>. Bonney Lake, WA: El Shaddai Ministries.

Blum, Julia.(2017). Israel Biblical studies.com. eTeacher Ltd. Ramat Gan, Israel.

Boyarin, Daniel. (2012). <u>The Jewish Gospels The Story of the Jewish Christ</u>. New York: The New Press.

Brettler, Marc Zvi. (2007). <u>How To Read the Jewish Bible</u>. New York: Oxdor University Press.

Cahn, Jonathan. (2016). <u>The Book of Mysteries</u>. Lake Mary, Florida: Front Line.

Cahn Jonathan. (2010). <u>The Paradigm</u>. Lake Mary, Florida: Front Line.

Frye, Northrop. (1981). <u>The Great Code The Bible and Literature</u>. New York: Harcourt Brace Jovanovish Publishers.

Frye, Northrop. (1990). <u>Words With Power.</u> Markham, Ontario. Viking Press.

Hershey, Doug. (2018). <u>Israel Rising.</u> New York: Citadel Press.

Johnson, Ken, Th.D. (2018). <u>Ancient Prophecies Revealed.</u> Middletown, DE.

Kushner, Aviya. (2015). <u>The Grammar of God</u>. New York: Penguin Random House.

Missler, Dr. Chuck. (2002). <u>Learn The Bible In 24 Hours</u>. Nashville: Thomas Nelson.

Nelson, Dwight K. (1998). <u>Built To Last.</u> Oshawa, ON: Pacific Press Publishing Association.

Panin, Ivan. (2014). <u>Panin's Bible Chronology In Three Parts</u>. Sidney, ME: New England Bible Sales.

Patriquin, Norm, J. (2009). <u>The Bible's Redemptive Pattern and Numeric Map</u>. Riverside, California: Xulon Press.

Rostand, Edmond. (1962). <u>Cyrano de Bergerac.</u> London: Heinemann Educational Books Ltd.

Sabiers, Karl, M.A. (1969). <u>Mathematics Proves Holy Scriptures</u>. Sidney, ME: New England Bible Sales.

Schnittger, Dr. David. (2017). <u>Zechariah: Israel and Her Coming King</u>. Southwest Prophecy Ministries.

Tozer, A.W. (2018). <u>The Knowledge of the Holy</u>. Lexington, Kentucky.

Tozer, A.W. (1989). <u>This World: Playground or Battleground.</u> Camp Hill, Pennsylvania: Christian Publications.

Whiston, William, A.M. (1998). <u>Josephus The Complete Works</u>. Nashville: Thomas Nelson Publishers.

about the author

Claudia Emilia Tagliasacchi Davison B.A., M.A.T, M.Ed., was born in Sampierdarena, (Genova) Italy. She came to Canada in 1967 with her mother and father (Vittorio and Vittoria) and two sisters (Rita and Letizia). Growing up in Chatham, Ontario, she attended the Salvation Army where she learned to sing and play the trombone, piano and guitar.

She wrote her first song at the age of seven. She will sing it to you if you ask. Since her first solo at age eleven, life has been full of performances, singing, bands and choirs. She directed her first choir at age nineteen and has since led church, school and community choirs at children, youth and adult levels for whom she has written original music.

At this time, claudia has three university degrees in language, literature and teaching, has studied conducting and holds advanced theory certification with the Royal Conservatory of Music. In her 30-year career as educator, she has taught English, French, Italian and Music as well as teen and adult Bible study courses.

As a composer and arranger, claudia has written over 200 songs. She has collected her best and most recent work in four musical CD recordings: darkness into light (2011), barely audible (2013), a thousand singing birds (2017) and comfort (2019).

In addition to her musical career, claudia has written four other books: *Fairy Tales the Magic Mirror (*psychological development and literary understanding of children into maturity*)*, *Unearthing the Hidden God* (Bible study journal), *Woven in Time* (a novel) *and Teaching the Books of the Bible* (interactive lessons and activities). She adds *a flower bent* to this list amalgamating her music and her writing. She explains, "my experience serving in the Salvation Army and my commitment to God have shaped me but also have released me to do what I find deep within my soul." This collection, *a flower bent,* is what can be found deep within her soul.